Antigua Guatemala

The city and its heritage

By Elizabeth Bell

Antigua Guatemala: The city and its heritage was based in part on the publication *Antigua Guatemala* by Elizabeth Bell and Trevor Long with photographs by Jacques and Parney van Kirk (Filmtrek, February, 1978). All research, updating and expanding of this publication, was done by Elizabeth Bell. © Elizabeth Bell.

Photographs:
Elizabeth Bell

Maps:
Archivo General de Indias

© First edition: February 1999
© Second edition: February 2001
© Third edition: June 2002
© Fourth edition: December 2003
ISBN 99922-706-2-4

© **Antigua Tours** by Elizabeth Bell
4a. Avenida Norte No. 25
La Antigua Guatemala
Tel/Fax (502) 832-0228
elizbell@gold.guate.net.gt

Printed in Guatemala by Textos y Formas Impresas

Dedicated to
Verle L. Annis
and
Roberto Aycinena Echeverría

Acknowledgments

The author wishes to thank, very specially, those who have inspired my work over the past 30 years of research. They include the Consejo Nacional Para la Protección de La Antigua Guatemala (1972–1986), the Centro de Investigaciones Regionales de Mesoamérica in Antigua, the International Centre for the Preservation and Restoration of Cultural Property in Rome and the Institute Nacional de Vulcanología, Metereología e Hidrología in Guatemala City. I thank Verle L. Annis (+), Guillermo Arzú (+), Rodolfo Asturias, Roberto Aycinena Echeverría, Enrique Barrascout, Margarita Estrada, Jorge Luján Muñoz, Luis Luján Muñoz, Christopher H. Lutz, José María Magaña Juárez, Carlos Humberto Quintanilla, William R. Swezey (+), María Cristina Zilbermann de Luján and many more who have encouraged me. Special thanks to Laura Woodward for editing the manuscript and Guisela Asensio for her work in creating this book. I also deeply appreciate the patience my children, Julio Ricardo Aceituno and Alexander A. Long, have shown.

Table of Contents

Brief History Santiago de Guatemala

Alvarado: The Beginning of an Era 3

Santiago de Guatemala 10

La Antigua Guatemala 16

Monuments

Introduction 29

Main Square or Plaza (1) 30

Palace of the Captains General and Royal Mint (2) 31

City Hall Palace (3) 36

Cathedral and Archbishop's Palace (4) 40

University of San Carlos (5) 47

Tridentino Seminary and School of the Indians (6) 48

Santo Domingo Church and Monastery (7) 51

San Francisco Church and Monastery (8) 55

La Merced Church and Monastery (9) 62

Escuela de Cristo Church and Monastery (10) 68

Stations of the Cross and El Calvario Church (11) 71

Capuchinas Church and Convent (12) 72

Santa Catalina Church, Convent and Arch (13) 76

Compañía de Jesús Church and Monastery (14) 77

Hermano Pedro Hospital (15) 81

Santa Clara Church and Convent (16) 82

La Recolección Church and Monastery (17) 88

San Jerónimo – Royal Customhouse (18) 90

El Carmen Church and Convent (19) 93

Santa Teresa Church and Convent (20) 94

San Agustín Church and Convent (21) 94
La Concepción Church and Convent (22) 97
Santa Ana Church (23) 102
Santa Cruz Hermitage (24) 102
San José el Viejo Hermitage (25) 105
San Sebastián Church (26) 106
Belén School and Churches (27) 107
La Candelaria Church (28) 108
Los Remedios Parish (29) 109
Santa Rosa de Lima Church (30) 110
Santa Isabel Hermitage (31) 110
Los Dolores del Cerro Church and Park (32) 111
San Lázaro Cemetery Church (33) 112

Museums
Museum of Colonial Art 115
Museums of Archeology
    and Colonial Art at Santo Domingo 116
Museum of Santiago (St. James) 121
Old Book Museum 122
Hermano Pedro Museum 123

Houses
Popenoe House 127
Doña Luisa's House 132
Casa de los Leones – House of the Lions 133
Casa del Conde 134
Landívar House 135

Fiestas and Holidays
Fiestas and Holidays 139
Calendar of Holidays 139

Physical Environment 151
Hill of the Cross 151
Volcanoes 152
Surrounding Towns and Areas 153
Ciudad Vieja 154
Jocotenango 155
San Antonio Aguas Calientes 156
San Felipe de Jesús 156
Santa María de Jesús 157

Historical Figures 161

**Chronological Record
of Damaging Earthquakes** 167

Recorded Fuego Eruptions 175

Bibliography 179

Map of Antigua 185

Brief History
Santiago de Guatemala

Alvarado:
The Beginning of an Era

On December 6th, 1523, under orders from the Conqueror of Mexico, Hernán Cortés, Pedro de Alvarado left Mexico City for the conquest of Guatemala. Leading a small army of 300 infantry, 120 horsemen, a hundred or so Mexican Tlascaltec warriors, and an odd assortment of light artillery, spare horses and ammunition, he was accompanied by two clergymen, Juan Godínez and Juan Díaz. The abnormal ratio of guns to priests was probably not left to chance. Despite Cortés's directive to Alvarado that he should "endeavor with the greatest care to bring the people to peace without war and to preach matters concerning our holy faith", Alvarado well knew the power of swords and guns in hostile and unknown territory. So he pursued his warring ways with great enthusiasm.

Indeed, for three years following his arrival in Guatemala, there ensued a series of massacres and destruction of such great proportions that no definite parallel can be drawn throughout the history of human warfare. Not to say that Alvarado's task was an easy one; quite the contrary, he endured tremendous hardships. Weighed down with heavy armor, Alvarado and his army traversed a hostile land. From the freezing temperatures of the mountainous highlands to the insect-infested malarial swamps of the subtropical forests, Alvarado and his men lost many skirmishes with their unforgiving environment, which often proved to be a far greater foe than the native population itself. But their religious zeal, their loyal, almost fanatical belief in Alvarado and, most of all, their avarice and greed carried them through every crisis. The ruthless Alvarado and company remained invincible.

On July 25th, 1524, after defeating the Mayas of Lake Atitlán with the enlisted aid of the Kaqchikel, Alvarado founded the first capital of "Santiago de Goatemala", in honor of Spain's patron saint, Saint James.

The city was conveniently located on the Kaqchikel capital of Iximché (near present-day Tecpán). In as few as six weeks, however, the friendly Kaqchikels became embittered by the extremely high tributes they were ordered to pay the conquerors and at the unjust treatment they received at their hands. They fled the city to regain their freedom in the sanctuary of the mountains, but to no avail; the conquerors began a war to wipe them out, this time with the aid of other tribes such as the K'iche's and Tz'utujils, as forced allies of the Spaniards. These were the very tribes that the conquerors had subjugated with the help of the Kaqchikels in previous years.

About this time, Pedro de Alvarado, informed that his enemies at court were plotting charges against him, sailed for Spain, leaving in his stead his brother, Jorge de Alvarado, acting as Captain General of Guatemala. Unhappy with the way things were going with the Kaqchikels, Jorge de Alvarado decided to move the capital from Iximché to the more peaceful valley of Almolonga, situated between the volcanoes Agua and Fuego.

There, on November 22th, 1527, the first formal capital of Guatemala was founded. The name of the previous capital, Santiago de Guatemala, was retained, not surprisingly, considering the credit given to Saint James for being the determining factor for the success of all the battles of Guatemala.

The mood in the beginning of this new settlement must have been one of great delight after the rigors of the highlands. Almolonga, "Place of Gushing Water", offered a year-round spring climate, good soil, clear water and the wooded slopes afforded a great quantity of building material.

The streets of the capital were laid out. All buildings focused around a main plaza. People erected crude thatched huts on land

4

compensated them according to their position in Alvarado's army. Immigrants too began arriving, though in small numbers. Construction progressed rapidly and, with the help of Maya labor, a cathedral, a hospital, schools and monasteries were erected. Cattle were brought from Spain, and farmers began to flourish in surrounding areas. By 1540, the city was on its feet and prospering.

During the fourteen years of the city's existence, Pedro de Alvarado was more the adventurer than the administrator. Suffering the loss of his first wife, Francisca de la Cueva, upon his return from Spain, he continued alone to Mexico. There, hearing exciting tales of gold and battles in Peru, he quickly returned to Guatemala, hastily built ships at the small port of Iztapa on the Pacific coast and, with what men he was able to muster, he set sail. Upon arriving in South America, he found himself at odds with Pizarro, who did not want to share the spoils of conquest. After accepting a payment of one hundred thousand *castellanos*, Alvarado returned to Guatemala. A short while later, he embarked on a second voyage to Spain where he married Beatriz de la Cueva, sister of his first wife.

Don Pedro de Alvarado, his lady, Doña Beatriz, and their huge entourage returned to Guatemala and, by most accounts, the next few years were spent in peaceful endeavor. In 1534 the new capital inaugurated its first cathedral and five years later Alvarado completed work on the Palace of the Captains General of the capital in Almolonga. By 1538 Alvarado had begun to construct a fleet to carry him and his men on an expedition to the Spice Islands (the Moluccas) as he had pledged to King Charles V. 1540 saw completion of his ships, and he set sail for Jalisco, Mexico to provision for the voyage. It was here that he was turned away from his original plans and persuaded, instead, to direct his fleet and forces toward Cibola (mythical seven cities, supposedly located somewhere in the southwest United States). Final preparations were at hand for the voyage a year later as word reached Don Pedro. Rebellious natives near Nochiztlán, Mexico, had besieged one of Alvarado's comrades in arms, Cristóbal de Oñate. Excited by the prospects of a battle, Alvarado rode to the rescue. But, in the course of the ensuing fight, a riderless horse tumbled down an embankment, mortally injuring the conquistador. Removed by litter to Guadalajara, Alvarado lingered a short while. When asked where he felt the most pain, the conquistador answered in anguish, "in my soul". He died on June 29th, 1541.

One year later Bartolomé de las Casas wrote of Alvarado:

> "Oh! How many orphans did he make, how many families did he rob of their sons, how many husbands did he deprive of their wives, how many women did he leave without husbands, how many adulteries and rapes and other acts of violence did he commit! How many did he deprive of liberty, how much anguish, how many calamities did the Indians suffer because of him! How many tears were shed, how many groans were uttered, how many people were left alone, how many were condemned to eternal servitude because of him! And not only Indians in great number but also unfortunate Christians who, in his company, perpetrated grave deeds, how many sins and detestable abominations! And may God have mercy on their souls and be satisfied with the vile ending He gave that tyrant."

Alvarado's death proved to be a foreboding omen of things to come. Within ninety days, a series of cataclysmic events occurred, leaving both his beautiful wife and daughter dead and the young capital in ruins.

That Doña Beatriz loved Alvarado there can be little doubt. She was only 22 years old when, after suffering the initial rumors, she received confirmation of her husband's death. Amidst a torrential downpour that had started the day before, she plunged the entire capital into prolonged mourning. The populace was shocked, then frightened, as the grief-stricken widow stained the massive palace inside and out with black clay. Rumors circulated the city

Fig. 1   Don Pedro de Alvarado

Fig. 2   Doña Beatriz de la Cueva

that such a blatant display of grief was just short of sacrilegious in the eyes of God, and surely some dreadful catastrophe would befall them. She compounded matters by substituting black for all crimson draperies and furniture in the palace, commanded that the city should mourn the death of her beloved husband for nine full days, and ordered all royal flags to be flown at half mast.

Day by day the intensity of the storm continued and large streams of water began flowing through the streets. The increasingly restless court plotted Doña Beatriz's arrest but she countered by having "every man connected with the plot put under arrest, regardless of rank". On the final day of official mourning, in an unprecedented move that testified to her ambition, she commanded the city's mourning, to appoint her in place of her husband to the highest position of the land, thus naming herself the first governess in the Americas. The following morning, September 9th, 1541, dressed and veiled in black, she signed herself into office as "*La Sin Ventura* Doña Beatriz". Immediately, in front of the royal clerks and all officials present, she boldly crossed off her name, leaving the name she would rule by, *La Sin Ventura*, the unlucky one.

The storm increased unabated. Rain and lightning lashed the small capital with all the powers of the heavens. Finally, at around midnight on the 10th, an earthquake added to the calamity and terror of the capital that was already fighting for its very existence. A massive quantity of mud and water loosened itself from the saturated sides of Volcano Agua and cascaded into the city knocking down everything in its path. In the black coffin-like palace, Doña Beatriz, her five-year-old daughter, and eleven women of the palace fled to the sanctuary of a small chapel recently constructed on the roof. Here they knelt and prayed for salvation amidst the terrified screams of the citizens caught in the devastation below, but their prayers this night went unanswered. The palace, constantly battered by the flood and heaving ground of the quake, could stand no longer and the roof and walls rained death on those huddled around the crucifix.

The short forty-hour reign of Doña Beatriz *La Sin Ventura* had ended.

Santiago de Guatemala

known today as
La Antigua Guatemala

After considerable debate, the survivors of the flooded capital of Santiago in the Valley of Almolonga agreed to abandon the devastated town in favor of a safer location no more than a few kilometers away. Here they would have all the advantages that made Santiago such an ideal location (water, good climate, fertile soil, and wood) plus the comfort of being a more secure distance from the destructiveness of the volcanoes.

Exactly fourteen years after the founding of the previous capital of Santiago a small procession marched to the new site in the Valley of Panchoy, "Valley of the Lake". Cords were stretched among the trees and grass to mark the streets of what would be considered a major architectural and historical gem of the Americas. Born in a cataclysm, cradled in calamity, it was destined to die in catastrophe.

The assignment of land began almost immediately while engineer Juan Bautista Antonelli carried out his task of designing the town. Antonelli may have not been in Guatemala at this time, but was probably in charge of engineering an "order of the New World" in the Spanish Americas on paper. Other cities had been incorporated from Maya villages or areas without formal direction. But, with a precise plan designed for five thousand inhabitants, he designed the new town in a perfect rectilinear pattern with avenues (*avenidas*) running north and south and streets (*calles*) in an east-west direction. He allocated adjacent areas for the Maya population who would act as beasts of burden during the construction of

10

the city. Despite all the careful planning, there remained a fatal flaw; the new town was built on top of a shallow water table, a factor that would prove unsafe during the violent stress of quakes.

Two years after the previous capital had faced its destruction the transfer to the new site was still barely underway. The City Council held its first meeting at the location of the City Hall Palace on March 10, 1543. This date is accepted as the founding date of the city. A few months later, the Church, dragging its feet in its reluctance for change, was transferred to the temporary cathedral in the new plaza. On June 13, it was publicly announced that the new capital would be known by the same name of its two predecessors (Santiago de Guatemala). The previously destroyed capital would henceforth be known as *Ciudad Vieja* (the Old City–actually located where San Miguel Escobar is today).

Santiago was most certainly a spacious town during its early years. The lots distributed to Spanish residents in 1541 took years to be fenced and the 16th century immigrants undoubtedly noted the lack of permanent structures. Even as late as 1566 when Philip II of Spain expanded the new capital's title to "The Very Noble and Very Loyal City of Saint James of the Knights of Guatemala" he could hardly have done so in recognition of Santiago's monumental character. Santiago was a remote city with neither mineral wealth nor rich spoils resulting from the conquest. It was primarily an agricultural center, making it all the more remarkable that conquerors of all classes should continue to settle there.

Friar Alonso Ponce, in his early account, reported the 16th century town as being of good size, populated by many noble but not wealthy people. Homes were built of rammed earth *(adobes)*, with some buttresses of brick and stone laid in lime mortar, and roofed with thatch or tile. Religious establishments, including three monasteries for monks (Santo Domingo, San Francisco and La Merced), one convent for nuns (La Concepción) and the Cathedral, had made their appearance. Ponce also notes two existing hospitals: one for Spaniards and one for Mayas.

Santiago was barely twenty years old when it suffered its first earthquake. From 1565 to 1586 six more shocks levied various damages on the city and dawned the ill-fated 200-year struggle for the capital's existence. Despite the need for reconstruction and repair that constantly plagued them, the early settlers proved to be a hardy and determined people. Overcoming onslaughts of disease, floods, and earthquakes, they developed a capital of importance that rivaled the splendid capitals of Lima and Mexico City, which suffered far fewer problems in their development.

As the population grew during the 17th century, so did the wealth and size of Santiago. The city limits were extended, and Mayas were again conscripted for both public and private works through the *encomienda* system. Much of the activity was in effect rebuilding, for already in the early part of the century the recurring quakes had resulted in damage and in some cases in total destruction of the existing buildings. All provisional buildings were torn down to build more formal architecture throughout this century.

In 1607, a great earthquake struck the city, and an edict was passed instructing the Mayas from surrounding communities, including some remote from the capital, to aid in rebuilding. While Maya slavery had been abolished in 1542, a labor tax had been established that proved to be essential in building and rebuilding Antigua's architecture. Devastating quakes hit again in 1651 and 1689, continuing the pattern of destruction and reconstruction. Each time the city met with disaster, new art forms in construction were introduced, incorporating a variety of Renaissance and Baroque as European art and architectural forms.

Religious orders gave much more importance to new building than did the Crown and, as a result, the number of ecclesiastical centers mushroomed. At the end of the century historian Fuentes y Guzmán recorded the names of 24 such centers; included were the Cathedral, ten religious organizations, three parish churches, five hermitages and four churches.

Along with the growing wealth of the churches many citizens increased their fortunes, though some used means less than honest, including the head of the government. As Friar Thomas Gage noted in "A New Survey of the West Indies, 1648: The English American":

"The President, though he have not the name and title of viceroy, as they of Mexico and Peru, yet his power is as great and absolute as theirs. His pension from the King is but twelve thousand ducats a year; but besides this, if he be covetous, he makes by bribes and trading twice as much more, nay what he list, as was seen in the Count de la Gomera... who departed in old age from Guatemala to the Canaries (where was his house and place of birth) worth millions of ducats."

Fortunately the city authorities did make attempts to meet the need for more adequate public services. Public fountains supplied the city water. Sewage was moved underground, and street repairs accompanied the embellishment of no less than eleven plazas throughout the city. The main plaza was the center for the market, pageants and bullfights, while religious festivities were held inside and in front of churches.

As if the calamities wrought by the earthquakes were not enough, the inhabitants were forced to contend with a series of floods and volcanic eruptions that added to their misfortunes. Although dikes had been placed on the banks of the Pensativo River after the flood of 1655, the river spilled over its banks in 1689 and 1762, causing severe damage. The rumblings and explosions of the nearby Volcano Fuego, only increased the residents' apprehensions but, as Gage writes:

"There was a time... when the inhabitants expected nothing but utter ruin and destruction, and durst not abide within their houses for nine days (the earthquakes continuing and increasing more and more) but made bowers and arbors in the market-place, placing there their idol saints and images, especially St Sebastian, whom they hoped would deliver them from that judgement, and for this purpose they daily carried him through the streets in solemn and idolatrous procession and adoration. But all the while I lived there the noise within the mountain, the smoke and flashes of fire without, and the summer earthquakes were such that with the use and custom of them I never feared anything, but thought that city the healthiest and pleasantest place of dwelling that ever I came in all my travels."

Somehow, surviving all its crises with nature, the young capital continued to thrive.

Santiago achieved both her architectural pinnacle and destruction during the 18th century. The reconstruction that had resulted from previous earthquakes continued and accelerated. Since the major quakes were spaced at relatively long intervals, it was only a short time before people forgot the horrors and agony that violently moving earth brings. Lulled into a sense of security, they would return yet again to whatever task was at hand. The primary chore was the reconstruction of shelter and, since the majority of religious buildings housed great numbers of clergymen and women, they too were rebuilt. Once the people were settled and permanent again, reconstruction began on churches, public facilities and government buildings. An excellent example of this happened in 1717. After a month of preliminary shocks, the September 29th earthquake, named after San Miguel, left the capital so severely damaged that serious consideration was given to moving it to another location. Yet just three years later began the largest building boom in the history of the capital. This "Golden Period" of development lasted for more than half a century despite further destruction from a severe earthquake in 1751.

This architecture, referred to as "Earthquake Architecture" by Pal Kéléman and "Earthquake Baroque" by Sidney Markman, is still earthquake proof today. In many cases structures were roofed with safer vaults and all new houses were limited to a single story. There were 31 ecclesiastical structures, and the main plaza had taken on a romantic character with the splendid cathedral, Palace of the Captains General and the City Hall Palace, towering above in majestic fashion.

By 1773 Santiago de Guatemala was at her zenith. Conflicting historical accounts place the total population of Santiago as high as eighty thousand. But, with due consideration to the size of the capital and a census taken right after the destruction of 1773, Christopher Lutz's tally of thirty-five thousand would be more exact. A population that included surrounding areas would have been higher than this count.

Early in 1773 tremors began to shake the city. By June the shakings and rumblings became so intense that the people abandoned the city in favor of open spaces. The Archbishop himself spent several nights in his private coach which had been wheeled to the security of the Main Plaza. Rains plagued those who feared to sleep under the shifting tonnage of tile roofs. Most work stopped, and Mayas refused to carry provisions into the town market. Towards the end of the month a period of relative calm lulled many people back into town. But it was not to last. On July 29th, St. Martha's Day, a massive jolt exploded under the city and the terrified populace rushed into the streets. Huddling with fear they murmured prayers for salvation. Ten minutes later, with a great rending and thunderous noise that deafened the horrified screams and shrieks of the masses a second enormous shock rocked the city. As the earth heaved and buckled for two terror-filled minutes that seemed an eternity, people were dashed to the ground. Crashing walls slammed into the streets as the air became thick with the choking dust of disintegrated mortar. Abruptly the convulsions ended. The sudden oppressive silence was pierced by the wails of the survivors. Santiago lay crippled, but for the warning of the first shock most would have perished. The city soon became pestilential; the unburied people and animals corrupted the air. The ceramic pipes to the fountains had ruptured, and water shortages added further to the suffering. Diseases of epidemic proportions ravished an already stricken populace.

On September 7th and again on December 13th, there were two more severe quakes, yet already temporary structures began to appear in patios and plazas as survivors struggled to get back on their feet. A conflict broke out between the University, the City Hall, the Church, and the Captain General as to whether the capital should be relocated. The majority of the population, including residents, the University, the City Hall, and the Church, maintained that the city should be rebuilt, but in the end the Captain General won. In September Martín de Mayorga abandoned the city, moving to the Valley of la Ermita, (present-day Guatemala City), some 45 kilometers away. In January 1774 they declared the new location the official capital. On July 24th of that same year "The Very Noble and Very Loyal City of Saint James of the Knights of Guatemala" was referred to as "La Antigua Guatemala" (the Old Guatemala) for the first time in an official document.

La Antigua Guatemala

The evacuation of Antigua was not a case of the populace trekking en masse across the mountains to establish their new capital. Rather, it was somewhat the opposite: a gradual departure of people and businesses embittered by governmental pressure. Many citizens, as well as ecclesiastical authorities, resisted the royal order that dictated immediate relocation. Primarily, it meant giving up real property for unimproved lots in the new city. This rebellion lasted almost four years until an order by the President of the district court made it illegal for anyone to continue living in Antigua. In the government's eagerness for a complete shift to the new site, they acquired a royal edict on July 28th, 1777. Moving must be completed and all property abandoned by March of the following

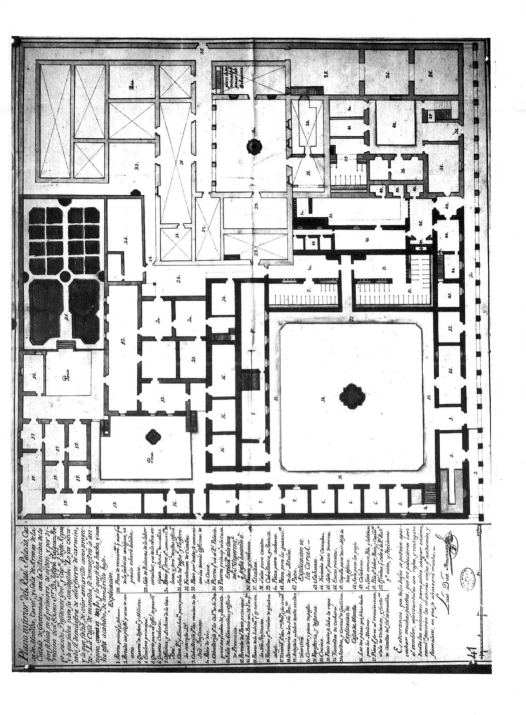

Fig. 3   Plan of the Palace of the Captains General

17

Fig. 4   Central Plaza
(*The Illustrated London News,* August 3, 1856)

year and that all of Santiago, now La Antigua, should be destroyed, leveled to the ground, after that date.

It is estimated that 14,000 of the 35,000 inhabitants moved to the new capital while probably half of the population relocated elsewhere including nearby provinces. This debilitated the socio-economic dynamics of Guatemala.

Maya labor was used to ravage the city during the years following the tyrannical decrees. The ensuing pillage left few doors, wood beams, locks, tiles, columns, furniture, art, or any other ornaments. The Captain General led the example by removing all valuables he could get on the backs of the mules and transported them to the new capital. Even the massive columns of the exterior arches were to be moved, but they proved to be too large and heavy for transport. As the time approached for the destruction of the remaining buildings, private homes were stripped and churches were gutted to furnish the new structures they were forced to build in the present day Guatemala City.

The city was never totally abandoned despite the efforts of the government and the wanton dismantling of buildings. Although the efforts of the Crown did more damage than the 1773 earthquake, Antigua was never completely razed. As decree after decree was published moving the evacuation date ahead, the Crown finally lost interest, somewhat appeased as the growth of the new capital gained momentum. The churches did eventually relocate as did many of the principal Spanish speaking families. But, not having much to gain by moving, the poorer inhabitants of the suburbs tended to rebuild their crude thatch and mud huts in short time.

Antigua became a place of vast ruin as time and nature worked their way against the remains of the monumental structures. Around 1830, the population began to grow once again when coffee was introduced in the area. Fortunately, it was generally easier to renovate the old houses than to build new ones and, as a result, it was possible to retain most of the character and beauty of the colonial period.

The 19th century brought few repairs to the battered abandoned capital but some efforts to restore houses are a result of the newly introduced coffee industry. Great efforts were made to carry out some restoration work on the Cathedral. While the entire colonial structure of the Cathedral took only 11 years to build, 30 years of restoration work only amounted to refurbishing only the entrance of the original Cathedral. Sculptures and paintings from other churches appeared in a haphazard way, unlike the original artwork. Money for further work was scarce.

José María Palomo y Montúfar appeared between 1850 and his death in 1855 as the most dynamic figure in restoration during this century. He requested original plans and maps from the archives in Guatemala City to restore Antigua to the way it had been in colonial times. Denied this request, he worked on the restoration of the City Hall Palace, La Merced Church and the Arch of Santa Catalina. He also built the public laundry fountain (*pila*), Tanque La Unión.

Efforts to rebuild Antigua at the end of the century include the work carried out on the front section of the Palace of the Captains General. In all instances, those who carried out the work had a desire to rebuild Antigua in its original manner. There was little interest in introducing new styles of the 19th century on the city's monuments.

Houses, however, did change a bit during this period. Neoclassical forms were added to domestic architecture: eaves were transformed to flat façades with moldings, some patios changed in shape and changes were made in the flower beds *(arriates)* and the empty homes came to life with beautiful furniture. In general, there was a conservative air in the atmosphere and people preserved their cultural heritage. Change was not as evident here as it seemed in other towns during the same time. With changing attitudes after the Revolution of General Justo Rufino Barrios, this desire to restore changed with the turn of the century.

As Antigua expanded in the 20th century, some house walls faced demolition for "improvements". In the 1930s there was little "real" consciousness about preservation. The fountain in the Main Square was torn apart to build a gazebo on top of it. The mermaids' heads were chopped off and these 18th century beauties were thrown in with the rubble in the Archbishop's Palace.

A handful of people became increasingly alarmed at the accelerating destruction of colonial structures in favor of more modern additions. The gazebo was eliminated one evening when a group of concerned academicians got together to begin the job of restoring the Plaza to its colonial flavor. In the early 1940s, architectural historian Verle L. Annis visited the city for an extended stay to document all the monumental structures, special homes and furniture. He requested that the Guatemala Government, through President General Jorge Ubico, give the colonial capital the distinction of "National Monument". A declaration was drafted with Ubico and residents in the old dining room of the Hotel Aurora. It was signed in the National Palace on March 30, 1944, making Antigua one of the first colonial cities in Latin America to be recognized as a monument. A special committee was set up to carry out restoration efforts. The government expropriated the main monumental structures, relocated squatters for their safety and cleaned the majority of the ruins. Some, including the church on the Santo Domingo property were not expropriated since they were considered too far out of the city center and not of much value. The committee was very active but funds dwindled and work became stagnant.

The mid-1960s brought the demolition of some colonial homes for new gasoline stations, "modern" hotels, dance clubs, movie theaters, and the like. Since there was no enforcement of true restrictions on new construction, citizens continued to destroy colonial homes. Some residents were outraged and prominent residents within the community, historians, architects and lawmakers joined to save Antigua.

In 1965 the VIII General Assembly of the Pan American Institute of Geography and History declared Antigua a "Monumental City of the Americas", which brought a new awareness of Antigua's importance.

A year later work began on a new project establishing protective laws for the city. In 1969, the National Council for the Protection of La Antigua Guatemala was formed by Congress, which approved the "Protective Law for the City of La Antigua Guatemala (Decree 60-69)". This specific law provides guidelines to preserve the city and a technical and administrative team to carry out the job. They began the tremendous task of preserving the colonial character of the city as well as maintaining the monuments. In the beginning it must have seemed impossible. Antigua and her monuments were buried under two hundred years of neglect. Trees and bushes grew so profusely among the great walls of the 17th century churches that it was difficult to tell where the roots ended and the dirt-filled structures began. Tons of dirt and rubble covered fountains and courtyards. The city streets were a jumble of neon signs, billboards and other trappings of the 20th century. But the Council kept working incessantly and slowly the proud colonial charm of Antigua surfaced once again. Technical work began in 1972 alongside the drafting of a Master Plan for the city. Work in the education of cultural heritage also became a priority to ensure a continuity of this work.

Then, tragically, during the early morning of February 4, 1976, another earthquake struck the city. In 39 seconds this earthquake became the worst natural disaster in the 20th century of the North American Continent, killing over 27,000 people and leaving more than one million homeless in Guatemala. The Council's four years of painstaking restoration seemed indeed puny compared to the destructive forces wrought in those few seconds. Many of the Council's recent accomplishments were left in ruin. Although burdened with the additional damages, they maintained their cam-

Fig. 5   Central Plaza 1875 by Eadweard Muybridge

Fig. 6   Drawing of Colegio Tridentino
by Roberto Aycinena Echeverría

24

paign for restoration. Today a quick glance at any portion of Antigua gives lasting testimony to the success of their continuing labors.

La Antigua Guatemala was included in UNESCO's World Heritage Site List in 1979. The impact of this would not be felt for a few years, however, due to the civil war at that time.

With support from Guatemalans, major work was carried out on the monuments in the 1980s. Donations from individuals and private corporations facilitated specific projects. A Restoration Workshop for Art was founded at the National Council for the Protection of La Antigua Guatemala. International technical expertise was well received over the following years. Local restorers began the enormous task of preserving collections of art in the churches and museums. Efforts in this area still continue in the workshop later set up in the Colonial Art Museum (Old University of San Carlos). The tasks were tackled: approval of building permits and sign licenses, education of schoolchildren in cultural heritage, registry of monumental property, restoration efforts, and instilling the importance of Antigua as a gem.

The war began to dwindle in 1986 and it was then that Antigua "all of a sudden came to life". After no tourism in the early 1980s, visitors began to flock and, with them, restaurants, hotels, shops, and e-mail cafés emerged. More importantly, the Spanish schools began to flourish. The first, Proyecto Lingüístico Francisco Marroquín, had been established in 1969 as a nonprofit institution. Each student has a private teacher and lives with a local family. It was this, and the following 65 schools that emerged in the 1990s that brought some economic development to Antigua.

While a few wealthy families from Guatemala City purchase houses, restore them and visit on weekends, most of the homes are occupied by *antigüeños* today. A simple look, however, only gives us a taste of the commercial part since all private homes are behind closed doors.

Despite earthquakes, floods and destruction caused by man, the entire city of Antigua has maintained a unique charm. The end of the 20th century brought too much traffic and, even too many people, worldwide. Antigua has not been saved from that part of globalization. Work still continues on improving traffic congestion, placing wires underground and much more. Many private associations are active in preservation efforts today. Antigua is blessed with a caring private sector.

Perhaps the essence of Antigua is found in its processions and traditions, perhaps in the morning view of the volcanoes, perhaps with Hermano Pedro at San Francisco Church, perhaps... those who visit Antigua experience a very special essence of the city's heritage.

Antigua is much more than a 16th century capital of Spanish America. Volumes could be written and still fail to capture her elusive ambience and charm. Yet a simple walk through the cobblestone streets saturates the senses with colonial flavor.

In a world where technology overwhelms creative energies, Antigua remains a refuge for artists and craftsmen alike, who continue to work in trades that have origins in the days of Alvarado. The pottery, woodcarving, metalwork, and ceramics are still exquisitely crafted with traditional techniques. The hand and the eye take preference over machines capable of mass production. As an art center, educational center, and monumental city, Antigua remains one of the most captivating places in the Americas; a living theater of cultural history.

Monuments

Introduction

Mankind, in his haste for development, has consistently destroyed most vestiges of his past. Antigua was saved from such a fate by one of the ultimate natural forces: the 1773 earthquakes severed the relationship between man and an already great city. Renovation, development, and destruction all stopped at the peak of colonial splendor. Antigua lay dark and quiet, preserved from the onslaught of modern technology. Mexico, Lima and other colonial cities were not as fortunate. Tear down the trees and three quarters of the monuments. Substitute parking lots for cobblestones, steel high rises for delicate façades and gray factories for lush plantations. Add several million people, smog, noise and congestion. Then you have the destiny all great capitals suffer. Antigua was spared from this. But, perhaps most of all, as it aged, it developed an elusive charm that remains intangible and defies description. Tile roofs, ornate doorways, fountains, façades and cobblestone streets all lend clues to the city's colonial character. The major influence, however, is her monuments. In varying states of majestic decay, they produce vivid images of a tumultuous past. A concise history of the colonial churches, convents, schools and monasteries follows. This makes no attempt to substitute words for an actual visit, but offers the reader a detailed reference to monuments that hold their interest. Monuments are generally ranked in order of importance, taking into consideration accessibility, size, detail, aesthetic value and history. This is nothing more than a general order for those who do not have the time to visit all of the ruins and should not be taken as factual sequence as opinions are greatly varied.

Main Square or Plaza (1)
(Plaza Mayor o Plaza de Armas)

In 1541, in keeping with the Laws of the Indies, the first cords laid out for the new capital designated the Main Plaza. Here were the beginnings of the great city that had previously existed only in men's dreams. In short time, foundations and the first streets took the place of taut cords. Fences, walls, and intricate façades slowly ascended replacing humble visions with an impressive reality. The east of the Plaza became dominated by the towering façade of the Cathedral with its adjoining Bishop's Palace. Architectural harmony became apparent with the construction of the City Hall Palace to the north and the Palace of the Captains General on the south side. The low-profiled businesses that bordered the west of the Plaza offered a view of two towering volcanoes: the active Fuego and the dormant Acatenango.

From its inception, the Plaza was a social center of no small importance. Since it was the very heart of the city, it was the stage for a variety of activities including bullfights, horse races, hangings, and whippings. The market firmly entrenched itself for centuries in the Plaza and became the gathering place for all to hear the latest news and spread the local gossip.

Despite the Plaza's well kept appearance today, its origins were rather dismal. For over 150 years, the Plaza was nothing more than dirt that became a quagmire during the rainy seasons. Water was first piped into the Plaza in 1555; six years later the first fountain was built, though it was placed off to one side where it was out of the way of bullfights and other activities. In 1704, cobblestones were laid, and the market began to flourish. But the entire area became so choked with vendors' stalls that the City Council issued an order demanding that all businesses be arranged in some systematic fashion so that carriages could pass. In 1738, the fountain was built anew in the center of the square, since the former one was in a bad state of repair due to the 1717 quake.

The present-day parklike appearance of the Plaza is the result of work done in the 20th century. The fountain now standing in the center of the Plaza was reconstructed about 1936. The main shaft had been broken when a gazebo was erected at the beginning of the century and several of its parts were scattered at some later date. The broken shaft was remade in concrete and the mermaids (*sirenas*) were recreated. The original mermaids are located in the Museum of Santiago and remain without their original heads, showing how the city was mistreated over the years, not as much by earthquakes as by its inhabitants.

Recent work on the Plaza included a complete renovation that began in 1991. Works were inaugurated in 1993. The Godchild Project began efforts to enhance the landscaping in recent years and currently maintains the Plaza's garden.

Palace of the Captains General and Royal Mint (2)
(Palacio de los Capitanes Generales y Real Casa de la Moneda)

Today, what was the main civil building in the region is a mixture of partly restored offices, ruins and subdivided residences. The front section includes offices for the Governor of the Department of Sacatepéquez, the National Civil Police, and the Guatemalan Tourist Commission. It is from the northeast corner that directions begin in Antigua (north, south, east and west). Avenues run north and south while streets, called *calles*, run east and west.

Colonial Guatemala encompassed Chiapas (Mexico), part of Yucatán, Guatemala, Belize, El Salvador, Honduras, Nicaragua and Costa Rica and it was from this building that they governed the entire area.

Although the main offices for the Captain General had been relocated in Gracias a Dios, Honduras between 1543 to 1549, there is no record of exactly where the royal offices were housed before the construction of the Palace began in 1558. The first construction was a two-story wooden structure that was erected on the southwest corner of the Main Plaza. It was here where the royal tax office and the department in charge of Mayas were housed, along with the other royal offices for Guatemala.

Bishop Francisco Marroquín sold his private house, located on the southeast corner of the Plaza, to the Crown in 1563, thus extending the Palace. It is evident that the Palace was not built according to any specific plan but was expanded and altered to meet the ever-changing needs of the Crown and Captain General. The lack of any logical arrangement of its services perfectly illustrated the latter.

The building was badly damaged in 1717 and buttresses were constructed to prop up some of its walls. However, reconstruction was never successfully carried out and, as a result, the building fared poorly in 1751. When the new Captain General arrived three years later, the building was still in a bad state of repair.

It was not until 1761 that funds were granted for the necessary repairs. The building with its façade with 54 arches was completed in 1764 although some construction continued. Eventually the Palace housed a variety of royal offices, including courts of justice, the royal treasury, chancery, council chamber, and a room for the royal seal and archives. Also, it provided working space for bookkeepers, scribes, and notaries and housed barracks for the guard, militia and a troop of dragoons. Stables for thirty-four horses of the Captain General were located inside the Palace as were cells for upper and lower class prisoners, a torture room, and a chapel for the condemned. All these services required various kitchens, laundry facilities, storage rooms and patios that met the needs of the Palace's numerous inhabitants. Its interior was lavishly decorated with woodcarvings, luxurious furniture and stately portraits of kings, queens, popes, archbishops and the like.

Fig. 7   Fountain in the Central Plaza

Fig. 8   The City Hall

The social importance of the Palace must not be overlooked. As distinguished visitors arrived at the capital, they were received ceremoniously by the royal officials and the court. On many occasions the ceremonies and celebrations were held in the Plaza while the Captain General and his family joined the ladies and higher officials of the colony in the corridor of the second story, where they overlooked the pompous festivities.

The Palace was probably slightly damaged in 1773 although damage reports may have been exaggerated to ensure moving the capital at that time. When it was moved to present day Guatemala City, the Palace was completely stripped of its original architectural adornments. The Captain General tried to take the stone columns to the new capital but they were too heavy for the mules to transport them. The columns remained in the back patio until later reconstruction efforts.

It was not until the late 19th and 20th centuries that any repairs were carried out on the gutted edifice. The façade and front section were rebuilt to their original appearance in 1890 by General don Manuel L. Barillas and engineer Ricardo Fischer. Architectural historian Verle L. Annis reported that in 1936 the governor's quarters were improved when the beautiful tile fountain from the kitchen patio at Santa Clara Convent was moved to the governor's patio. Debris was cleared from various courtyards and, unfortunately, two beautiful colonial fountains were demolished to make way for sports areas in the east section. In 1942 other repairs were carried out.

The Guatemalan Tourism Commission restored the northeastern corner (including both stories) with efforts by former Director Álvaro Arzú and the National Council for the Protection of La Antigua Guatemala in 1981 under the direction of the Conservator of the City, architect José María Magaña Juárez.

A project for the Palace's complete restoration was prepared in 1997. This elaborate project requires healthy funding. It did, however, allow Governor Enrique Montano to remove the Army

Reserve Offices from the battered Palace in December of the same year.

The Royal Mint (2)
(Real Casa de la Moneda)

Located on the southwest corner of the Palace of the Captains General, this building is currently used for tax collection and phone facilities.

Due to the scarcity of coins during the 18th century, the Crown granted permission for the minting of coins in Santiago. In 1733 construction began on the Royal Mint, located on the same block of the Palace of the Captains General. It was here that *macacos* were coined and stamped with the Spanish Coat of Arms. These coins may now be seen in some museums.

City Hall Palace (3)
(Palacio del Ayuntamiento)

The city offices that occupy most of this Palace give services to some 70,000 *antigüeños*. City services include water, birth registration, *cédulas* (Guatemalan identification cards) and, since 1998, payment of property taxes. The Museum of Santiago (see "Museums") is housed in the west portion and main patio.

Although the first meeting of the City Council was held on March 10, 1543, there is little known about the various reforms and repairs that were carried out on the *Casa del Cabildo* or *Casa Consistoriales* as it was named then. While reports note the addition of pillars in 1629 and iron railings some fifty years later, whatever structure existed at that time was completely reformed in 1695. It was this patchwork structure that was badly damaged in the 1717 quake and faced repairs within a year or two.

Fig. 9   Cathedral façade

Fig. 10   Figures inside the ruins of the Cathedral

In 1740 construction of a new building from the ground up was undertaken and inaugurated by the City Council with great pomp three years later. This Town Hall included spacious rooms for the City Council, the city "Jail of the Poor" and a chapel for those unlucky prisoners who spent their last moments in peace before facing the gallows in the Main Plaza. Its construction was superior. While the rest of the city was damaged by the 1773 quake, it required only minor repairs. The building was abandoned in 1779 when the capital moved to its present location.

With the introduction of coffee and efforts by Corregidor José María Palomo y Montúfar, the Palace was restored to its original elegance in 1850. Iron railings on the corridors were also added. Its main façade is a dignified two-storied arcade with stone columns on a base raised a few steps above the level of the street. It is one of the few buildings in Antigua that has the appearance of a veneer of large square blocks. Yet, upon closer inspection of the side façade, each block is made up of smaller stones. Walls are four feet thick.

As in colonial times, the City Hall housed the local police and prison quarters until the 1950s, when that portion of the building was restored to house the Museum of Santiago. The remainder of the building continued to function as the City Hall with a Council Chamber until it was badly damaged in 1976. The National Council for the Protection of La Antigua Guatemala restored the Palace once again in the 1980s. Today the City Hall Palace is vibrant with meeting areas and also houses the offices of the Municipal Tourism Police which were introduced by Mayor Víctor Hugo del Pozo en 1997.

Cathedral and Archbishop's Palace (4)
(Catedral y Palacio Episcopal)

The front part of the colonial Cathedral is active while a major portion of this magnificent structure remains in ruins and may be accessed from the south side. The parish part of the Cathedral has a collection of art that dates back to colonial times, in part, and to more recent *retablos* and sculptures. The collection of paintings illustrating the Apostles (1680) is of particular interest. The processional figures from the 17th and 18th centuries are also of great interest. They include the Cristo del Perdón (recently retired from processional life), Jesús Nazareno, and the Señor Sepultado. Brotherhoods, *hermandades*, of which this parish has two, store processional floats in the ruins. These *hermandades* are in charge of the processional figures in the church and all of the activities that focus around them.

Visitors may get a close-up view of the fascinating stabilization work of the massive walls. Other highlights in the ruins include the colonial burial vault which is used as a Maya prayer area today. It has concrete sculptures added in 1943. There are other burial vaults accessible to the public at the south entrance.

While the ruins of the present-day Cathedral are reminiscent of the second construction, completed in 1680, the first structure was built of adobes and thatch. Due to the lack of funds, work began slowly in 1542. Bishop Francisco Marroquín used what materials he could salvage or sell from the damaged Cathedral in the previous capital (San Miguel Escobar) to continue work. In 1545 the Crown allotted funds for the Cathedral in the new capital. Two years later, the income from the *encomiendas* of the Spanish conqueror, Pedro de Alvarado and his wife, Beatriz de la Cueva, which had been accumulating since their deaths, was designated for building costs. The construction remained incomplete throughout the century, however, despite the elaborate carving of a wood roof and tile that replaced the thatch. After suffering damages dur-

Fig. 11   Detail of Cathedral façade

Fig. 12 *Señor Sepultado* inside San José Cathedral

ing the 1583 earthquake, parts of the roof fell as late as 1600 and repairs were constantly being made until 1616. It is unusual that one of the main churches in Spanish America should have such modest construction as late as the 17th century when other churches in Guatemala already had vaults or domes. Indeed, the workmanship was so poor, and the building was in such a constant state of disrepair, that it was finally decided to completely demolish the structure and start anew.

In 1669, under the direction of Captain Martín de Andújar, work began on what would be the most majestic edifice in colonial Guatemala. Captain Andújar was dismised early on due to the difficulty he experienced in building vaults. Then, for eleven arduous years, under the direction of Architect Joseph de Porres, Mayas, accompanied by oxen and wheelbarrow, labored as the townspeople gazed at the creation of this work of art from the market in the Main Plaza. The entire Cathedral was raised on a stone platform extending one-city block in size. The façade closely resembled what it looks like today although some reconstruction and repairs are evident. Its low and heavy quality shows that the builders were aware of seismic risks. Through illustrations from the "London Illustrated News" (1856), we appreciate the original bell towers (probably demolished after 1880) but only our imagination may recreate this entire jewel.

Descriptions vary tremendously as to its elaborateness. All sources agree, however, on the grandeur of the baroque colonial style. Papal seals, Royal Coat of Arms, archangels, angels, Saint James's emblems, and finely wrought bronze medallions were further embellished with decorative sculpture in plasterwork executed with lime mortar over brick. The altar was intricately carved and inlaid with mother-of-pearl, ivory and silver. The Cathedral's numerous images and paintings were the work of the best colonial sculptors and artists of the time: Quirio Cataño, Alonso de Paz and Antonio Ramírez Montúfar among others.

Although the Cathedral withstood the 1689 quakes, the 1717 quakes weakened the walls and columns (little repair was actually required) and, as a result, the 1773 quakes may have proved disastrous.

While some reconstruction was attempted, it was apparently done informally since, in 1818, little work had been accomplished. In 1821, an active church was deemed necessary and the restoration of the entrance was completed after years of efforts and few funds. Works of art were brought in from other churches in Guatemala and, at the beginning of the 20th century, modest altars *(retablos)* were created.

The present-day Cathedral, now the parish of San José, occupies the entrance of the original building including the baptistery and only two chapels. No attempt has been made to capture any of the majestic touches of its predecessor. The damaged San José Parish badly needed repairs after 1976. A special donation and government funds approved by former Head of State Oscar Mejía Víctores funded restoration work carried out by the National Council for the Protection of La Antigua Guatemala beginning in the early 1980s. Current works that embellish the altars *(retablos)* are being carried out under the direction of Father Juan Carlos Córdova and the author of this publication is sponsoring the restoration of the 1680 paintings of the apostles through restorer Margarita Estrada.

The ruins of the Cathedral were partially cleaned in the 1940s in preparation for the city's declaration as a National Monument (1944). Excavations in the burial vault underneath the main altar produced human remains. An academic discussion resulted at this time as to whether these were, indeed, the remains of Pedro de Alvarado, Doña Beatriz, Leonor de Alvarado, Bishop Francisco Marroquín and other colonial figures who had been given the honor of being interred beneath the Cathedral's main altar. The exhumed remains were placed in a box and housed in the local courthouse until the early 1980s. At that time, the author was present when those who had carried out the excavations and forensic doctors gathered to open the box. With tape recorders in hand and great ceremony, the box was opened. Those present immediately acknowledged that the remains were not those they had placed there some 40 years prior and, in fact, were not human remains at all! It appears that the remains had been tampered with over the years. They reported that Bernal Díaz del Castillo, the fine 16th century historian, had requested to be buried in his armor. Those carrying out the excavations were prisoners and placed these remains, covered in wrinkled metal *(chatarra)*, in the truck and off they went to the countryside *(barranco)*. Other remains were lost over the years.

The ruins of the colonial Cathedral are undergoing stabilization, or consolidation, work by the National Council for the Protection of La Antigua Guatemala. Though much of the vaulting has fallen, elaborate stucco figures adorn the tops of the remaining columns. In the east part of the ruins, steep stairs lead to a burial vault or crypt, modified to be a chapel possibly around the early 1940s. Today, candles placed by Maya worshippers light the chapel. Five other burial vaults were excavated after 1976, and throughout the 1980s, yielding a number of human remains. Four of these vaults are accessible and clearly show that these were not "meeting places for the nuns and the monks."

In 1998, work began under the direction of the National Council for the Protection of La Antigua Guatemala to create replicas of all of the brick and plaster sculptures. This work continues today.

Archbishop's Palace (4)
(Palacio Episcopal)

While various portions of this elaborate gem are used as private dwellings, public toilets and the Casa de la Cultura, the remains of the cloister are open to the public with access from the south entrance of the ruined Cathedral. The Palace has faced destruction from earthquakes that plagued the city for the last two centuries but remains of the elaborate mural paintings that covered its interior are still evident on the broken columns and cloister walls. These patterns, applied with stencils and painted while the plaster was still damp, remain as some of the finest examples of mural paintings from colonial times.

The Palace's history dates to the times of Bishop Francisco Marroquín who moved his residence from the corner of the Royal Palace to this location when the capital was very young. It will never be known what his house looked like since it was rebuilt and enlarged between 1683 and 1702. The inauguration of the current building took place in 1711 after completion of cloisters, a magnificent library, offices, fountains, dining area, kitchens, servants' quarters and stables.

On December 16, 1743, Pope Benedict XVI signed the necessary bull to elevate the rank of bishop to archbishop, and investiture of the first archbishop took place in Santiago two years later. The archbishop was the highest ecclesiastical official in colonial Guatemala and was housed here until 1775. It was from here that Archbishop Pedro Cortés y Larraz opposed the relocation of the capital during 1773–1774.

Probably the last building to be abandoned in the 18th century, archeological excavations in 1981 proved that squatters inhabited one section after that time. A hearth and previous Maya burial were unearthed, recorded and reburied, by William R. Swezey and the National Council for the Protection of La Antigua Guatemala.

Old-timers report bull fights and circuses giving life to the still standing cloister in the 1930s and 1940s. With consolidation work carried out on the elaborate stucco and mural paintings by the National Council for the Protection of La Antigua Guatemala in 1975, but without the necessary structural reinforcement, the gorgeous arcade collapsed in 1976. Provisional roofing protects the mural painting until funds are available for its restoration.

46

University of San Carlos (5)
(Universidad de San Carlos)

The old university has housed the Museum of Colonial Art (see "Museums") since 1936, when it was established officially. Its cloister arcade is perhaps the most ornate in Antigua and offers one of the best examples of interior plasterwork. The elaborate doorway on the façade dates from 1832 and the beautiful fountain that enhances the patio is probably not original and may have been moved here from another location.

Preoccupied that advanced education was restricted to friars in convents, Bishop Marroquín and the Dominican Order worked out an agreement to found the School of Santo Tomás de Aquino and the bishop willed money and land to the school shortly before his death in 1563. It was not, however, until 1620 that the school was established and classes in philosophy, theology, medicine and Latin were offered to the sons of Spanish speaking inhabitants. The Colegio de Santo Tomás had accumulated sufficient funds from a series of gifts from distinguished citizens to warrant a request for university status. The Council of the Indies, however, denied their requests. In 1646, a wealthy member of the community offered a donation of enough funds to support five chairs of study if the King and Pope gave their permission within four years. It was not, however, until thirty years later that the King approved the royal decree founding the University of San Carlos. It was located on the property occupied by the Dominican Monastery. The delay in approval was partially due to the arrival of the Jesuits in Santiago and their requests to establish the university.

University classes began in 1681 with seventy presumably anxious students, and studies were offered in a classical Renaissance education: law and medicine, philosophy and theology, and a Maya language (Kaqchikel), in addition to subjects already in the curriculum. The Pope finally confirmed the establishment of the

Royal and Pontifical University of San Carlos and gave it the same rights and privileges as the universities established in Mexico, Lima and Salamanca.

After 1751, the University's housing was rendered in a disastrous state of repair. The Rector of the Tridentino Seminary generously donated the houses adjacent to the Seminary and one of the most attractive buildings in Santiago was erected, under the direction of royal engineer Luis Diez de Navarro. While most of the city suffered some damage in 1773, the University suffered very little damage at all. While the University moved to the new capital, the old building was one of the first monuments to be refurbished in the 19th century. It was renovated as a primary school in 1832 (note the entrance).

Tridentino Seminary
and School of the Indians (6)
(Colegio Tridentino y Colegio de Indios)

Adjacent to the old university, the Tridentino Seminary has been subdivided for private residences and alterations have taken place for more than two centuries. Parts remain in an excellent state of conservation including the very elaborate stucco doorway that faces the south side of the Cathedral. It may be studied from the street and is, indeed, the most elaborate in town.

Philip II approved a decree in 1592 that seminaries should be founded in all New World dioceses in accordance with the rulings of the Council of Trent. It was not, however, until six years later that the Seminary of Our Lady of Ascension, or Tridentino, was founded with fifteen students. Its present location was ceded a century later and work began to erect a fine new building during the middle of the 18th century. A few years later, the Tridentino building was enlarged behind the University to provide rooms for Maya students to attend the Seminary on scholarships, and an oratory

Fig. 13   Old San Carlos University

Fig. 14   Santo Domingo view of Volcano Agua

was built in the southern section of the University. Since the Seminary did not have the necessary funds, these rooms were built at the expense of the Rector in order to comply with a royal decree stating that all seminary schools had to establish scholarships for the sons of Maya chieftains *(caciques)*.

The Tridentino Seminary and the School of Indians shared one of the most beautiful buildings in the city. Not only is it one of the few that was designed as a complete structure rather than a building that grew with additions, but it shows skill and advancement in the area of planning. The Church auctioned the property in 1860 and different families have acquired it since that date. One family acquired a property deed for the section of the building located on the corner in 1900 when the State was improving property registration.

Santo Domingo Church and Monastery (7)
(Iglesia y Convento de Santo Domingo)

As an excellent example of "sustainable tourism", the Hotel Casa Santo Domingo, with its restaurant and cultural center with beautiful museums, provides needed jobs. Visitors may now see sections of the friars' bedrooms, dining area and kitchens. The church, excavated in 1995, has been cleared of a 16-foot layer of rubble. Excavations of burial vaults provided the project with a true "treasure", the burial vault of the Calvary, a pristine mural painting from the 1680s with a scene of a Crucified Christ, Mary, Mary Magdalena, two thieves, and canopy with the sun and the moon. Discovered in September 1996, this is the finest treasure found in Antigua in post-colonial times. Special visiting times were immediately established to view this work of art. Attractions also include the Colonial Museum and the Archeology Museum.

The Dominican Order *(Orden de los Predicadores)* arrived in Guatemala in 1529. They were allotted extensive sites first in the

Valley of Almolonga, where the previous capital was located and, then, in Santiago in 1542. Santo Domingo became the largest and the richest monastery in the new capital. Its church was completed in 1666 although some work may have continued. Enormous twin bell towers held ten bells. One of its towers displayed the first public clock, brought to Santiago in 1553. Throughout the church and monastery was a wealth of colonial art. A Dominican friar built the magnificent fountain in the main cloister in 1618. Thomas Gage enhanced prior descriptions through his writings about his travels to Guatemala. He described the church as being the most sumptuous and well finished in Guatemala up until 1680 when the Cathedral was completed. The monastery housed more than 80 friars. These friars were also in charge of the first school of higher education (Colegio de Santo Tomás de Aquino). This school became the University of San Carlos in 1676 and remained on Dominican property until 1763. The friars' quarters included quarters, beautiful gardens, patios, an elaborate water system, baths and lavish rooms.

In 1717, 1751 and 1773, earthquakes damaged the church and monastery but greater damage occurred when the townspeople used the ruins as a quarry for other housing construction in Antigua during the 20th century. In fact, the high school, Instituto Normal Para Varones Antonio Larrazábal, was built on the old atrium of the church at the beginning of the 20th century, with building materials from these ruins. It was so seriously damaged in the 1976 earthquake that it was completely demolished.

Restoration work was carried out on the area that included a portion of the friars' bedrooms and the kitchen to house a magnificent private residence. Dr. Edwin Shook and wife, Virginia, purchased the property in 1970. They spent five years cleaning out the debris from this section of the Dominican monastery. Shook, an archaeologist, also carried out 53-foot excavations (looking for the bottom of the lake that was once located in the valley) and discovered pre-Hispanic ceramic that dates to around 3,000 BC.

Fig. 15   Santo Domingo fountain

Fig. 16   Santo Domingo altar at front desk

They embellished the property with a library, garden, living room, kitchen, and guest bedroom. The dining room was placed in the old kitchen-bath area and they added a master bedroom. The Shooks sold the property in 1989 to a private corporation that transformed the house into a restaurant, tore down the master bedroom to build "the old wing" (1992) and acquired adjacent properties to carry out extensive restoration work of great interest. More wings have been built around the archeological remains of the monastery, after painstaking efforts were taken to preserve colonial remains. The construction company, owned and managed by the Castañeda family from Guatemala City, is engaged in a hands-on effort to "rescue" this part of colonial heritage. Work also included the consolidation of the main cloister where a copy of the original large fountain is located in the center. (The original fountain was relocated to the entrance of town and then to the Alameda de Santa Rosa in the 1930s so that those removing building materials would not also remove it!) The ruins of the monastery, with its burial niches and waterways, have also been unearthed.

In the late 1990s the Colonial Museum, the Archaeological Museum, and two fascinating burial vaults were open to the public. Today, Casa Santo Domingo is spectacular!

San Francisco Church and Monastery (8)
(Iglesia y Convento de San Francisco el Grande)

The San Francisco Church is one of the most frequently visited by Guatemalans and foreign tourists alike. The reconstructed church, with its altars and colonial paintings is one of the most lavishly decorated in Antigua. Here lie the remains of the venerated Hermano Pedro de San José de Bethancourt, and many faithful continually pray to him for a favor or miracle. The plaques on the wall near the north chapel testify to the miraculous powers that Hermano Pedro holds (see "Historical Figures"). Museo del

Hermano Pedro (located on the south side of the transept) has Hermano Pedro's personal belongings on display in a miraculous state of conservation (see "Museums").

Arriving in 1530, the Franciscans were one of the first orders established in colonial Guatemala. The civil authorities assigned them an income from 120 Maya villages. They were among the first to make the move to Santiago where they built a small adobe church, located where Escuela de Cristo is today. This church was badly damaged in the 1565 quake and alms were still being collected ten years later for the construction of a new one. Work began in 1579 and San Francisco soon became a cultural center for the region. The Franciscan School of San Buenaventura taught theology, canonical law, philosophy, experimental physics and mathematics. It included a beautiful chapel, library, music and art rooms and printed materials on its own press. Many learned men and great artists in the country, famous painters and sculptors such as Villalpando, Merlo, de Liendo and Paz created works of art for this center.

Work continued throughout the 17th century. The wood ceiling in the church, built in 1674, was so richly carved that it had no equal in the colony. The massive three-story hospital was enlarged in 1684, only to face damage during the quake five years later. Reconstruction began immediately and the church was enhanced with a large main altar, lavishly sculpted saints, and five gilded side altars.

Although work continued after that date, in 1702 San Francisco was inaugurated. The complex eventually covered four city blocks. Severely damaged by the 1717 quakes, all of the church arches cracked, the bell tower was partially destroyed and the new infirmary was damaged. Unfortunately, during the reconstruction buttresses were raised and this proved to be a major factor in the destruction caused in 1773 since these were not attached properly to the walls but were built next to them. The church and monastery were left in ruins even though the Chapel of the Third Order, where

Fig. 17   Church of San Francisco
(*The Illustrated London News,* March 12, 1859)

Fig. 18   San Francisco Church today

Fig. 19   Detail of San Buenaventura on
San Francisco Church façade

Fig. 20   Sculpture of processional Jesus of Nazareth
at San Francisco Church

Hermano Pedro was later buried, remained intact. This chapel always remained open to the faithful and never fell into ruin.

The church, which lay in a ruined state, was rebuilt in the 1960s due to the efforts of José García Bauer, engineer Oscar Martínez Dighero, and many others who joined to recreate a church in honor of Hermano Pedro. While engineers rebuilt the church, they failed to give it its original proportions and flavor: none of the art there today is originally from San Francisco. Without the original elaborate paintings, sculptures and relief decoration that were characteristic of the colonial structure, it acquires a somewhat bare aspect. It has, however, acquired a very special tone of its own. This is attributed to Hermano Pedro. While the reconstruction efforts saved the church from further destruction, words are difficult to find to convey the very special atmosphere inside San Francisco. The most important activities revolve around the previous burial location of Hermano Pedro in the Chapel of the Third Order, and those praying at the current burial location. Hermano Pedro was beatified in 1980 and is scheduled to be canonized in July 2002.

During November of each year, Fray Augusto Ramírez Monasterio is particularly remembered. He was declared a martyr by Pope John Paul II during his visit to Guatemala in 1992 for his efforts and death at the hands of the national police in 1983. His remains are in the Chapel of the Third Order.

Many of the gilded altars and sculptures brought from other churches in the 1960s add to this ambience. The Christ figure, located to the north side of the altar, is exceptional. Known as *Cristo de Tusa* (corn husk Christ), this sculpture was made in Guatemala in 1550 out of corn husks and covered with paper mache. It is believed that the Mayas placed figures inside the corn husks and we know that the Spaniards used Maya writings for the paper mache. The altar behind it dates possibly from the 17th century and was restored by Margarita Estrada in 2001–2002. The altar on the south side of the main altar is the most beautiful in Antigua today.

It dates from 1690. The virgin, however, must date from the 1960s. While she is usually dressed in her traditional light blue color, sometimes the little old lady who dresses her makes more colorful dresses with bright pinks and reds. This shows the importance of both hands-on activities with the sculptures, and faith.

Points of interest in the ruined monastery include frescoes and paintings of the skeletons and priests found in the ruined portion of the monastery. There is also a magnificent view of the city and the volcanoes from the second story of the ruins.

La Merced Church and Monastery (9)
(Iglesia y Convento de Nuestra Señora de las Mercedes)

La Merced Church holds regular church services and is famous for the brotherhood's processions of Jesus of Nazareth on Palm Sunday and Good Friday. The fine processional sculpture is on display to the south side of the altar until Lent when it is placed in a more prominent location.

The Fathers of La Merced *(mercedarios)* were one of the first orders to establish a monastery after the conquest of Guatemala. Their first building in the previous capital (San Miguel Escobar) was still incomplete and unoccupied when that capital was destroyed. Reluctant to abandon their property, they were not immediately awarded land in the new capital. It was not until the intervention of Bishop Francisco Marroquín that the City Council assigned them a site on the northern edge of Santiago.

For over two centuries the Fathers struggled to erect a formal church. Both a combination of perhaps poor workmanship and successive earthquakes hindered their efforts. Finally, in 1749, a new architect, Juan de Dios Estrada, was put in charge. With a keen awareness of seismic destruction that was greatly reinforced by the 1751 earthquake, Estrada built the new structure in a low and

Fig. 21   La Merced Church

Fig. 22   La Merced plaster detail

Fig. 23   Door carving on entrance to
La Merced Monastery

Fig. 24   La Merced fountain

squat form. Walls were constructed of great thickness and buttresses were added to impart strength. Windows were kept small and placed unusually high, keeping the mass low and concentrated. The inauguration took place in 1767. The ornate church façade with its exquisitely detailed stucco, called *ataurique,* remains one of the finest example of plasterwork in the city.

Six years later the massive 1773 earthquake struck the capital. La Merced survived almost intact, a credit to Estrada's abilities. But six months later a second shock rocked the city, leaving the previously weakened monastery damaged. La Merced was abandoned. A new church with an almost identical interior was constructed in the new capital and the paintings, carved altars and all works of value were moved to the new structure where they can still be seen today.

The present appearance of La Merced Church has changed very little since 1773. It was restored with the efforts of Corregidor José María Palomo y Montúfar in 1850. The Jesús Nazareno was moved from Santa Cruz Hermitage to La Merced Church in 1853. The church was severely damaged in 1976. The National Council for the Protection of La Antigua Guatemala was in charge of an excellent restoration project. In 1997 the church was repainted with the traditional lime-based yellow paint characteristic of colonial times. The El Volcán company in Guatemala City financed the historical research and paint for this project. While some suggested that it looked like a "birthday cake", the patina will soon develop to enhance this colonial church.

To the left of the main façade is the entrance to the monastery. Its ruined cloister features the largest fountain in the city and is thought to be the largest in Spanish America. The perimeter of its base almost fills the entire cloister. Four bridges radiate from the central island to the corners of the cloister walls. Its middle column and bowl are almost twenty feet high and are decorated with elaborate stucco designs.

Two dates are inscribed on the stone cross standing in front of the church. On the shaft below a heart-shaped blazon appears with the date 1688 and on its base the date 1765. The dates and a study of the material suggest the cross is a composite of three different structures.

The fountain located to the right of the church façade originally stood in the main cloister of the San Francisco Monastery. In the 1940s, the large lower basin was removed in pieces and reassembled where it stands today. Here it served as a water tank with a bust of Fray Bartolomé de las Casas on a pedestal in the center. The original bowl and supporting columns were finally reunited with the basin after Antigua was declared a National Monument (1944). Though there is no exact date of the fountain's construction, it was probably built in the latter part of the 18th century since improvements were made on San Francisco's cloister at that time.

Escuela de Cristo Church and Monastery (10)
(Iglesia y Convento de la Escuela de Cristo)

Under the care of the Franciscan Order, Escuela de Cristo remains famous for its processional activities during Lent and Holy Week. The procession with the Crucified Christ *(Señor Sepultado)* on Good Friday is among the finest in the world. While the church lacks significant altars, it contains some magnificent art, including the venerated life-size Crucified Christ entombed in glass and another Christ figure. Quirio Cataño, who lived near the church between 1575 and 1595, may have sculpted both wooden sculptures. The cloister is used today by an active Franciscan Seminar.

This has one of the longest histories among the religious establishments. The hermitage of Vera Cruz was founded by Bishop Francisco Marroquín in 1533 in the previous capital (San Miguel Escobar) and took possession of the little church and house that the Franciscans had built for temporary use on the southeast side

Fig. 25   Ceramic lion on the dome of La Merced

Fig. 26   Escuela de Cristo Church

of Santiago. This hermitage remained under Franciscan care from 1543 to 1664, when a group of friars joined together to found the institution known as the Escuela de Cristo.

In 1689, the Escuela became the Congregation of San Felipe Neri and the friars of this order accepted missions to the most remote parts of the country. These first years efforts were very restricted because the gifts and endowments that they had expected to receive failed to materialize. Their troubles were further increased when their old church was ruined in 1717. In 1728, they received financial support to rebuild their church and architect Diego de Porres completed the new church two years later. Ten years later, the monastery was in bad condition and only five friars and two novices remained in residence. The 1773 earthquake damaged the cloister but left the church less damaged than most others in Santiago.

Extensive reconstruction was carried out during the 1940s and 1950s and the church and seminar are active today.

Stations of the Cross
and El Calvario Church (11)
(Estaciones del Vía Crucis
e Iglesia de El Calvario)

El Calvario Church is open to the public for services and houses an impressive, although decaying, collection of colonial art. The Stations of the Cross that lead from San Francisco to El Calvario only open for religious festivities today, particularly during Lent.

Beginning at San Francisco Church with number one, the remaining thirteen Stations of the Cross were originally determined by measuring the one thousand three hundred and twenty-two steps that Jesus took on the way to crucifixion. Wooden crosses initially represented the stations; these eventually evolved into elaborate paintings showing the appropriate scenes. Vaulted chapels were erected at every station in 1691. The last stations are found inside the gate of El Calvario.

The first church and gate were built in 1618–1619 but did not survive the 1717 quakes. Immediately afterwards, building started again, and the gate and church which stand now were completed three years later.

The stone cross in front of the gate has the date 1688 inscribed on its base. It is likely that it replaced a wooden one which was erected in 1618 and designated the site where the church was to be built.

One of the most beautiful fountains from colonial Guatemala is located in the *alameda* in front of the church and was built in 1679 with approximately three thousand pesos donated by a member of the City Council. Its massive pedestal and bowl are ornately decorated with stone relief images of angels and flowers.

The Stations of the Cross and church were used by the Franciscans and were used continually during the Good Friday celebrations until 1773. The chapels were partially restored in 1942 for use during celebrations for Antigua's four hundredth anniversary. Efforts to restore them again were undertaken by the Fundación para la Conservación de La Antigua Guatemala in the late 1990s.

Capuchinas Church and Convent (12)
(Iglesia y Convento de Capuchinas –
Nuestra Señora del Pilar de Zaragoza)

Partially a ruin today, the old convent houses the offices for the National Council for the Protection of La Antigua Guatemala. Its unique tower is well worth a visit. Capuchinas is a favorite monument in Antigua.

Four convents for nuns had already been established in Santiago when the Capuchin nuns of Madrid petitioned the King

Fig. 27   Capuchinas Church

Fig. 28   Arch of Santa Catalina

for an establishment of their own. The City Council opposed the building of the convent, reporting to the King that the country was too poverty stricken to support another. But, as was the case with the Recollects, the City Council lost. By royal decree on May 5, 1725, the Capuchin nuns received approval for their new convent, provided that the convent authorities limit its population to twenty-five nuns, five of whom should be lay members. The decree to establish a convent came as somewhat a surprise to the City Council since their protest had been lodged as a formality in recognition of an earlier royal decree that prohibited the founding of additional cloistered establishments. Probably the decisive factor in the King's suspension of the latter decree was that all previous convents in Santiago required a dowry for entrance. The Capuchin nuns would do a service by allowing many good but destitute women entrance into religious life without a dowry. And so the Convent and Church of Nuestra Señora del Pilar de Zaragoza (nicknamed Capuchinas due to the nuns' brown habit) was approved.

Approximately one year after the decree was published, the first five nuns arrived in Guatemala as founders. They temporarily resided in private houses until a formal convent and church could be built for them. By 1726 work had already started. The structure we admire today was completed in 1736 and built by the fine Guatemalan architect, Diego de Porres. It was the last convent for women to be built in Santiago de Guatemala. The two-story cloister originally housed a number of services for the cloistered order, including administrative offices, workrooms, bedrooms, dining room, kitchens, hot water baths, and an infirmary with a dining room and kitchen located on the second floor. Women from the colonial capital were allowed to stay in infirmaries in convents since the two hospitals were for men.

Without dowry endowment, life in the Capuchin convent was harder than other convents in the capital. The nuns dedicated their time to chores and prayer. These included taking care of orphans and abandoned children, a hospital for women and schools for boys and girls.Once they accepted their vows, they were not allowed to leave the convent except when earthquakes threatened the convent and the bishop ordered them to seek open shelter.

The 1751 quake did partial damage to the structures and as a result of the nuns' petition the City Council aided in repairs.

Abandoned in 1774, it remained mostly unattended for 70 years. It was sold to a family in 1850. They tore down the tile roof to dry coffee on the second floor. This may have helped in its preservation, since appropriate drains were installed on the second floor.

Today, as one of the best-preserved monuments in Antigua, Capuchinas has in recent years been the subject of a number of independent studies. The focal point of these has generally been the round towerlike structure situated to the north of the main cloister. It is known as the Tower of Retreat for the Novices. From the sub-floor of this tower a massive column rises to support the higher floor which has a circular patio encompassed by eighteen cells, each with a door facing the center. The sub-floor, designated as a storage room for food, has a very broad room that revolves about the supporting column. Incorporating a 133-foot circular wall are fourteen small recesses with a small vent at the top, and several have small stone rings protruding from the sides. The 14 niches were designed as Stations of the Cross, each with an air vent for candle smoke. With its cells (bedrooms), hot baths and refined sewer, the tower remains unique, with no counterpart in Spain or the Americas.

Santa Catalina Church, Convent and Arch (13)
(Iglesia, Convento y Arco
de Santa Catalina Virgen y Mártir)

Santa Catalina Church may be viewed from the Street of the Arch and the old convent may be visited from the businesses housed amidst the original convent of "Santa Catalina Virgen y Mártir".

Due to the crowded conditions of Santiago's first convent, La Concepción, a demand arose for an additional cloistered convent for women. In 1609 four nuns from La Concepción were awarded permission to establish the convent of Santa Catalina. By 1631 the original number of four had grown to fifty-two. As the church and convent were completed, the nuns obtained permission to build an arch joining additional property across the street from the convent itself. The arch was hollow with steps on each side and, within this elevated tunnel, the nuns were able to cross over to the school without being seen, thus complying with cloister regulations.

In 1697, the convent reached maximum capacity with one hundred and ten nuns and six novices. Within fifty years, however, the enrollment would decline in size to include only 49 nuns and one novice. The reduction in population was most likely due to the proliferation of religious establishments. The arch, though damaged, remained standing, precariously defying earthquakes, until reconstruction took place in 1850, due to the efforts of Corregidor José María Palomo y Montúfar. The clock tower was probably added at that time.

The convent presently houses a hotel and the old school which was located across the street has been modified for private residences and a bed & breakfast.

Compañía de Jesús Church and Monastery (14)
(Iglesia y Convento de la Compañía de Jesús)

Antigua loaned the old Jesuit complex to the Spanish government for restoration in 1990, through the Cooperación Técnica Española. Restoration of its three cloisters allows the building to be used as an Inter-American Cultural Training Center and for cultural activities. Visitors may enter to see contemporary exhibits and cultural activities.

In 1607 two Jesuit fathers arrived in Santiago to establish the "Colegio de la Compañía de Jesús". The Jesuits lived in a thatched structure while building was carried out on the formal church and they inaugurated the new structure in 1626. Twenty years later the Jesuits were graced with a bequest of thirty thousand *pesos*. This money was used for the construction of a new church with adjoining monastery and school. Properties for the church were acquired from the heirs of historian Bernal Díaz del Castillo. Much of this was destroyed in the 1695 earthquake and yet another church, which stands today, was built after that time. The new school and church withstood the 1717 quake but suffered severe damage in 1751. The Jesuits asked for four thousand *pesos* to make the necessary repairs and evidence suggests that their request was granted.

At its height, La Compañía de Jesús was one of the most impressive religious structures in Santiago. Covering one city block, the complex encompassed a church, monastery, school and a house for spiritual exercises. Besides three cloisters, there were libraries, classrooms, assembly rooms, administrative offices, refectories, and kitchens. The school awarded degrees in philosophy, grammar and rhetoric. Rafael Landívar, who was a young student at the school, became Guatemala's foremost colonial poet.

In the 18th century an anti-Jesuit movement took root in Spain and King Charles III, who was an avid supporter of the movement, ordered the expulsion of all Jesuits in the Spanish New World. Notification of the order reached the colonies in June 1767. Early in the morning of July 1st, under armed guard, the fathers of the Compañía left their property, traveled to the coast, and sailed from Guatemala, never to see the country again.

Several attempts were made to utilize the empty structures but the building was still vacant when the 1773 quake struck. The complex remained abandoned for several years; it finally housed a textile factory in 1865.

The Public Market was moved from the main square to occupy the monastery in 1912. The complex suffered heavy damage

Fig. 29　Compañía de Jesús
(*The Illustrated London News,* March 12, 1859)

Fig. 30   Compañía de Jesús, new and old

in the 1976 quakes and the market was evacuated to its present location in *La Pólvora.*

Extensive efforts through the National Council for the Protection of La Antigua Guatemala included clearing the area and stabilizing the church. With funds from the Guatemalan Government and the United Nations Educational, Scientific, and Cultural Organization (UNESCO), the restoration of elaborate mural paintings in the church was completed during the 1980s. The Cooperación Técnica Española began restoration efforts in 1990. These continue today.

Hermano Pedro Hospital (15)
(Known as San Pedro Hospital)
(Obras Sociales del Hermano Pedro u Hospital San Pedro)

Las *Obras Sociales del Hermano Pedro* (Hermano Pedro Social Works) use these facilities for a number of clinics and hospital wards that serve the poor. Founded in different houses in 1980, the Obras received permission to use the hospital in 1985. They have received private donations to rebuild the old hospital, initially due to the efforts of Fray Guillermo Bonilla. Information about this charity organization may be obtained at the entrance to the hospital, located to one side of the church. The church holds religious services today and is also open to the hospital's patients.

The hospital's history dates back to colonial times. With funds from the Cathedral taxes, it was built for clergy members and was inaugurated in 1663 under the administration of the brothers of the public hospital, San Juan de Dios. In 1668, the Cathedral was temporarily moved to the hospital's church until construction was completed on the new Cathedral in 1680.

Immediately after the 1773 quakes, the small hospital staff was under tremendous strain since they had to attend the ecclesiastical members along with all other male patients because the public hospital had been damaged. At that time, the name of the hospital was changed to San Juan de Dios. It was later moved to Guatemala City.

The brothers of the public hospital continued to maintain the abandoned hospital in Antigua until 1865 when the Capuchin nuns took charge of the building. Four years later, the Sisters of Charity of the Congregation of Saint Vincent de Paul took charge. In memory of the founder of the Hospital of Belén, Hermano Pedro de San José de Bethancourt, the hospital was known as Hospital del Hermano Pedro. As the only public hospital in Antigua, it was severely crowded with the dying and injured after the February 4th, 1976 quake. Two days later, a second earthquake struck the city and the damaged hospital was immediately evacuated. It was eventually relocated in an old government hotel on the edge of town, Rancho Nimajay, and then to its newer location outside of town.

The church and hospital façades, although altered in detail in 1869, remain of interest and may be seen from the park in front of the hospital. The stucco is not in character with the 18th century churches. Also, one of the most interesting baroque doorways is located on the hospital's southeast entrance, to the rear of the church.

Santa Clara Church and Convent (16)
(Iglesia y Convento de Santa Clara)

Santa Clara remains in ruins today and is open to visitors. The church and cloister have gardens and, on a clear day, a picturesque view of the Volcano Agua in the background.

The founding nuns came from Puebla, Mexico in 1699. Three convents for nuns had already been established in Santiago. A large endowment bequeathed by a widow and generous donations for private citizens facilitated the founding of the new order. Within three years, the formal convent and church were completed.

82

Fig. 31　San Pedro Hospital entrance

Fig. 32   San Pedro old hospital entrance

Fig. 33   Santa Clara Church side entrance

Fig. 34   La Recolección

The convent was two stories high and embraced the usual cloisters with a kitchen, refectory, infirmary, workrooms, and enough cells to house forty-six nuns.

The church was well planned. Confessionals were built into the inner church walls and the convent faced the structure so nuns could enter and leave either building unseen. Roofed with wood and tile, as was the early convent, it contained both upper and lower choirs connected by a spacious stairway. Five elaborate altars decorated its interior. The main altar, richly carved with wood figures, was the dominant feature.

The short, squat construction technique utilized after experience with previous earthquakes proved ineffective when the massive 1717 quake damaged the church and convent. The nuns moved their residence to the small town of Comalapa while attempts at rebuilding were carried out. Since the land holdings of the order were damaged in the earthquake, leaving the nuns with less than half of their usual income, the completion of the new structure was not realized for a full seventeen years. When the new church and convent were inaugurated on August 11th, 1734, the nuns found themselves blessed with a building even more spacious than before. The quarters were pleasant, the infirmary expanded, vaults replaced the wood roofs and a cell was added for demented nuns. One problem had not been contemplated. The architect, Diego de Porres, seemed to have been unaware of the nuns' construction regulations when designing and building. The church was designed with a front entrance only. This was later sealed to comply with the necessary building regulations. The convent entrance was added so that the beautiful façade may not be seen from a distance and, thus, part of the convent was rebuilt in the process.

The 1773 earthquake left the church and convent damaged. Abandoned, it was not until 1874 that the church dome collapsed. A house was built in an open area in front of the convent and squatters occupied the interior of Santa Clara until 1944. At this time, it became national patrimony. The 1976 quake spared the ornate façades and beautiful fountain. Many of the second story arches collapsed. It remains among the most fascinating sights in Antigua today. The National Council for the Protection of La Antigua Guatemala carried out consolidation work on this magnificent monument throughout the 1980s.

La Recolección Church and Monastery (17)
(Iglesia y Convento de La Recolección)

By far the most impressive, massive ruins of the colonial capital, La Recolección is also one of the largest found in Antigua. Visitors are captivated by the massive blocks of ruin *(tetuntes)* that lie in the church.

In the late 16ᵗʰ century, Santiago was a capital with an increasing population. Churches, monasteries, convents, chapels, and hermitages in different stages of construction competed with other factions of city construction for space. In fact, when two Recollect friars came to Santiago to establish a monastery in 1685, the City Council flatly refused their request. The Council stated that there were already far too many religious orders for the citizens to support. Furthermore, if they were granted this approval, the Council feared it would lead to more religious requests.

But the Recollects persisted despite the adverse local opinion until authorization was approved and they had their own temple replete with "domes, statues, altars, and ornaments and dwelling in keeping with all of these." In 1700 they succeeded in obtaining a writ signed by the Crown ordering that the monks not be impeded from founding their convent. The writ was presented to the local courts one year later and the duly impressed City Council awarded parcels of land in the suburbs of San Jerónimo outside the city limits. Not to be at odds with the Crown, the City Council even went as far as to take part in building a temporary thatched church structure.

The cornerstone of the church was laid on September 8, 1701 and throughout the years the cloisters, refectories, cells or bedrooms, study rooms, infirmary and pharmacy, choir and music rooms were added. In 1715 the church was completed and the inauguration took place on May 23, 1717. Ironically, a few months after the inauguration, Santiago suffered a major quake and the church and monastery were significantly damaged. Reconstruction began quickly and even greater magnificence resulted. The church became one of the largest in Santiago. The church and monastery were again damaged in 1751 but it is not clear to what extent. The fatal blow came 22 years later in 1773.

Although nothing more than a massive skeleton remains, the ruin was not totally abandoned. During the ensuing years, an odd assortment of people and animals used the cracked hulk of stone and mortar for various purposes. Destitute squatters huddled among its walls and corridors; pigs and other domestic animals rooted and pecked among huge pieces of vaults and walls that lay strewn about. Sections of the once proud monastery were carted off into the surrounding area for use as walls and fill. At one time, both corridors were used for sports and local fairs but perhaps the final degradation came early in the 20th century when a boat-shaped swimming pool was constructed in one of its cloisters! It was later removed by the mayor.

For centuries, rising from the midst of tons of scattered masonry and roof, stood a massive yet fragile arch that miraculously survived nature's destructiveness. An aspiration to innumerable poets, writers and artists, its image can still be seen on countless paintings, postcards and photographs. Although it defeated quake after successive quake, time finally took its toll and all who knew the arch of La Recolección were saddened by its collapse on February 4th, 1976.

The house to the rear, known as the Casa de Recoletos, was restored by the National Council for the Protection of La Antigua Guatemala and the Organization of American States in the 1980s. For many years, a workshop for the restoration of colonial art, under the direction of Margarita Estrada, tackled the tremendous task of restoring paintings and sculptures that had fallen into a poor state of conservation. The restoration efforts on the structure did, however, effectively preserve the building.

San Jerónimo – Royal Customhouse (18)
(San Jerónimo y Real Aduana)

San Jerónimo provides a backdrop for cultural and social activities, highlighted by the local children's ballet each year in November. Open to the public, the grounds are now well kept and include benches for quiet contemplation of the ruins.

In 1739 the order of La Merced petitioned the authorities for permission to found a school. They argued that, since the Dominicans and Franciscans had their own schools, it was only fair that they too have one. Work began almost immediately, and the imposing two-story structure was completed within twenty years. Only two years after its inauguration, the school was ordered closed because the Fathers of La Merced had not received a building permit from the Crown. The king also issued orders for its demolition. These demands were eventually rescinded and His Majesty approved the building for use as a royal customhouse in 1765. Within two years, the structure contained living quarters for the customhouse officials, a full company of dragoons, and stables for 150 horses. Plans were drawn up for an extension of the military barracks but not carried out due to the decision to move the capital.

The excellent construction of the building is still apparent. Though there is no trace of the stables, one can still see the origi-

Fig. 35　San Jerónimo fountain

Fig. 36   El Carmen Church

nal arrangement of the building. The cloister faces a beautiful octagonal fountain and the school's kitchen is adjacent to the cloister walls to the south. Its original roof is remarkably well preserved as are most kitchens in Antigua. The National Council for the Protection of La Antigua Guatemala did consolidation work in 1975 and again after 1998.

El Carmen Church and Convent (19)
(Iglesia y Convento de Nuestra Señora de El Carmen)

One may still view the nave of the church from the street but the convent has been reconstructed into private homes.

Permission was granted to build Our Lady of El Carmen in 1638 and the inauguration took place the same year. This suggests that either construction had begun before permission was granted or that the building was adapted from a previous structure. In any event, it may have been poorly built, for it was severely damaged by the 1651 quake and reconstructed. A new and larger temple was inaugurated in 1686 but was also damaged during the 1717 quakes. The third church on this site was completed after considerable expense in 1728. It was one of the finest in Santiago and was noted especially for its orators and music.

The church's interior was one of the most elaborate in the city because of its six side altars and very fine main altar. The church also had an intricate brick tile floor, decorated wood railings and burial vaults beneath the nave. The church and convent were badly damaged in July 1773 but major destruction took place on December 6th of that year when the vaults, dome and bell tower collapsed. The beautiful figure of Our Lady of Carmen enhanced the façade until she fell in the 1976 quake. Consolidation work during the 1990s helped to stabilize the church. Work continued in 2001–2002.

Santa Teresa Church and Convent (20)
(Iglesia y Convento de Santa Teresa de Jesús)

The elaborate façade, designed by architect Joseph de Porres can be seen today by visitors but only the less fortunate contemplate the convent's interior since it houses the city prison.

Two convents for nuns had already been founded in Santiago when Bernardo de Obando, the founder of the Escuela de Cristo, brought three of the barefoot Carmelites from Lima, Peru to establish their own order.

Financially backed by a Lima philanthropist and his wife, the formal convent and church were built from 1677 to 1687. Joseph de Porres, the renowned architect of the new Cathedral, composed the plans of the church. Though there were only eighteen nuns in the convent, the cloisters were not modest. The two-story structure was severely damaged in 1717. The terrified nuns constructed thatched shelters in the courtyard and continued to use them for some twenty years. The convent was then restored to its former condition. The 1773 quake destroyed the vaults of the church but the badly damaged walls and façade remained standing. The façade of the convent, as well as the convent and the church, survived all earthquakes, including the 1976 quake. Consolidation efforts began in the late 1990s under the direction of the National Council for the Protection of La Antigua Guatemala.

San Agustín Church and Convent (21)
(Iglesia y Convento de San Agustín)

San Agustín may be viewed from the street and the convent houses stores and a hotel today.

Although the Fathers of San Agustín arrived in Guatemala as early as 1610, it was not until 1657 that they completed work on their new church and convent. The church had a single nave vaulted

Fig. 37   San Agustín Church

Fig. 38   San Agustín façade detail

throughout and was furnished with paintings by the famous artist Antonio de Montúfar. Although little is left today, the church and convent occupied the entire eastern side of the block, and the gardens and orchards extended to the Alameda de Santa Lucía. The convent was a large cloister surrounded by an impressive two-story arcade. After the damage caused by the 1717 quakes, reconstruction began slowly due to the lack of funds. After some twenty years, the King authorized the city government to help rebuild their church. This was damaged in 1751. The rebuilt building, inaugurated in 1761, was damaged again in 1773 and, as a result, the Augustines were the first order to leave Santiago for the new capital. The 1917 quake further damaged the ruins when the dome collapsed. As late as 1938 anyone who wanted rubble or dressed stone could purchase it from this ruin, adding to the destruction and the former cloister was used as a stable yard for oxen. The 1976 quake took its toll when the remaining portion of the church's upper choir collapsed. Some clearing of debris was carried out in the 1980s.

La Concepción Church and Convent (22)
(Iglesia y Convento de la Inmaculada Concepción de María)

Suffering from the fate of most ruins in Antigua with subdivision, the Church may be viewed by visitors while the convent remains in ruins, or completely demolished, and private property owners have rebuilt very little on the property. Although the convent was the first and largest in Santiago, only the massive church ruins and Doña Juana de Maldonado's quarters remain today. The church offers little of architectural interest, is devoid of much ornamentation, and offers no hint of the fine altars and paintings that it once contained. The private cloister of Doña Juana, however, is remarkably well preserved.

Religious life in Antigua during the late 17th century was by no means limited to a handful of devout men struggling in poverty to convert the pagan Indians to "a civilized faith." As the custom of that time was to send one's second son into a religious order, the Church membership included the offspring of many noble and rich families and the churches avidly accepted the wealthy into its growing ranks.

While there were no strict rules on one's daughters joining the convent, many young women chose to do so. For over fifty years, there was no convent for women, until 1578 when an abbess and three nuns arrived from Mexico to found the Convent of "La Inmaculada Concepción de María". No limit was set on the number of nuns allowed in the order and, as a result, the convent expanded to massive proportions. In its greatest expansion, La Concepción contained well over a thousand women, not all nuns, but nuns, servants and young children (mostly orphans and abandoned children) who were brought up and taught to work by the nuns. Since the majority of nuns came from the leading families of the colony and paid exorbitant dowries, the convent was one of the richest in colonial Guatemala.

A city within a city, covering more than six blocks, the convent was ripe with all the conflicts and politicking of a palace court. One of the sisters, Doña Juana de Maldonado, financed both by her wealthy father and allegedly a lustful bishop, built her own luxurious quarters in the convent, replete with galleries, private garden, hot baths and half a dozen servants. Thomas Gage refers to her in 1625:

> "[A]bove all she placed her delight in a private chapel or closet to pray in, being hung with rich hangings, and round about it costly *láminas* (as they call them) or pictures painted upon brass set in black ebony frames with corners of gold, some of silver, brought to her from Rome; her altar was accordingly decked with jewels, candlesticks, crowns, lamps, and covered with a canopy embroidered with gold; in her

Fig. 39   La Concepción bath

Fig. 40   San José el Viejo Church

closet she had her small organ, and many sorts of musical instruments, whereupon she played sometimes by herself, sometimes with her best friends of the nuns; and here especially she entertained with music her beloved the Bishop. Her chapel or place of devotion was credibly reported about the city to be worth at least six thousand crowns, which was enough for a nun that has vowed chastity, poverty, and obedience. But all this after her decease she was to leave to the cloister; and doubtless with this state and riches she would win more and more the hearts of the common sort of nuns, till she had made a strong party, which by this may have made her abbess. Thus is ambition and desire of command and power crept into the walls of nunneries, like the abominations in the wall of Ezekiel, and hath possessed the hearts of nuns, which should be humble, poor, and mortified virgins.

"But besides this one nun, there are many more, and also friars, who are very rich, for if the city be rich (as is this) and great trading in it, they will be sure to have a share. Great plenty and wealth hath made the inhabitants as proud and vicious as are those of Mexico. Here is not only idolatry, but fornication and uncleanness as public as in any place of the Indies."

The convent was considerably damaged during the 1717 and 1751 earthquakes and La Concepción suffered a steady decline in numbers. In 1773 the convent again lay damaged.

Almost all the original convent was quarried away up until 1970. Many used the brick and stone to rebuild Antigua over the years. While it remains in private hands, very little of the property has been developed.

Santa Ana Church (23)
(Iglesia de Santa Ana)

In use today, Santa Ana is a parish for a lively neighborhood. The *hermandad* (brotherhood) participates with a procession during Lent and the neighbors are active with other traditional celebrations. Santa Ana's Day is celebrated on July 25th.

Historian J. Joaquín Pardo reports that there was a small chapel servicing the southeast corner of town before 1541 and, at that time, it was elevated to a hermitage. If this is true, Santa Ana is the oldest church founded in the Valley of Panchoy. In 1690, it was described as being a beautiful little church located in a neighborhood inhabited by forty Europeanized Kaqchikel families. Forty years later, taxes were collected from the local inhabitants for rebuilding the church. It has an ornate baroque façade, possibly last rebuilt after the 1751 quakes.

In 1917 and 1928 the church suffered severe damages and required considerable repair, completed in 1929. A more extensive renovation was completed in March 1965, with funds provided by Matilde Geddings Gray. Restoration efforts took place again after the 1976 quake when, in the early 1980s the Franciscans received funds to repair the roof. The façade is quite lovely.

Santa Cruz Hermitage (24)
(Ermita de la Santa Cruz)

This elaborate façade provides an impressive background for cultural festivals including the Paiz Cultural Festival sponsored every other February by Fundación Paiz.

Originally founded under the administration of the wealthy Dominicans, Santa Cruz retains one of the most elegant façades in Santiago. Built on the southeast border of the capital in 1662, it became the parish church for a neighborhood of almost thirty Span-

Fig. 41   Santa Cruz Hermitage

Fig. 42   Santa Cruz Hermitage detail

ish-speaking Kaqchikel families. After severe damage of the first structure during the 1717 quake, a number of the more prosperous Kaqchikel families received permission from the City Council to rebuild. The new structure was first used for services in 1731 but was not fully completed until 1746 when the City Council was again petitioned for construction funds. Partially damaged by the 1751 and 1773 quakes, the ornate façade remains almost intact. The church interior is less profuse in decoration but a careful examination of some of the windows and nave reveals sporadic concentrations of excellent stucco detail.

A small amphitheater was constructed in front of the church in 1969.

San José el Viejo Hermitage (25)
(Ermita de San José el Viejo)

Viewed from the street, the neighboring Spanish school that has the same name and from the patio at the Hotel Antigua, this short, squat façade is a favorite.

In 1740 a movement began to build a small chapel where the carved image of Saint Joseph, sculpted by Alonso de Paz, could be properly displayed. Construction began two years later when the city officials reported that sufficient alms had been collected for the building. In 1744, a license was formally requested to legalize the work already done but the Crown was angered at the delayed petition and not only closed the hermitage but ordered the building torn down and the Government Fiscal fined.

Although construction stopped and the statue was temporarily moved to Santa Lucía Church, the partially built structure was not torn down but was extensively damaged in 1751. In 1759, a request for reestablishing religious services was brought before the civil authorities. This action was successful and the new building was completed in 1761. The hermitage was inaugurated the following year and the sculpture was returned. Finishing touches were carried out in 1763. It probably did not suffer much damage in 1773. While some of the vaulting fell, it was sound enough to serve as a temporary convent for the Carmelite nuns of Santa Teresa.

San José el Viejo was occupied during the 19th century and reportedly housed a tannery and used as a barn in the 1930s and 1940s. Fundación G&T financed consolidation work during the late 1990s with the supervision of the National Council for the Protection of La Antigua Guatemala. Its unorthodox baroque façade is one of the most beautiful in the city today.

San Sebastián Church (26)
(San Sebastián)

San Sebastián may be viewed from the street and plaza located in front. Unfortunately, due to the February 4, 1976 earthquake, only a fraction of San Sebastián remains today.

The church was originally founded as a hermitage in 1566 and was erected on the hill of San Felipe to the north of Santiago. This original site proved too remote and was moved to more level ground at the bottom of the hill in 1582.

About forty years later, when Thomas Gage entered the city on the road from Guatemala City which came through Chimaltenango, he wrote:

"I had not rid on above a mile from the church of Jocotenango, when the hills and mountains seemed to depart one from another, leaving a more spacious object for the eye to behold, and a wider valley to wander in. The fame of that city from Mexico and Chiapas has raised up my thoughts to conceit of some strong walls, towers, forts or bulwarks to keep out an aspiring or attempting enemy. But when I came near and least thought of it, I found myself in it without entering through walls, or gates, or passing over any bridge, or finding any

106

watch or guard to examine who I was. I passed by a new-built church standing near a place of dunghills, where were none but mean houses, some thatched, and some tiled. On asking what town that was, answer was made me that it was the city of Guatemala (Antigua) and that, being called San Sebastián, was the only parish church of the city."

The church suffered only partial damage during 1773 and it was not until a severe earthquake struck in 1874 that the roof caved in. For centuries, the ornate stucco façade and walls constantly withstood earthquakes.

In 1973–1974, the National Council for the Protection of La Antigua Guatemala carried out some work on the elaborate plasterwork found on the façade. But, after months of painstaking work, the 1976 quake took its toll. It was perhaps the most damaged façade in Antigua at that time. Many restoration experts acknowledged that consolidation of this ruin was indeed too difficult due to the severe structural damage it suffered and adjacent traffic. Due to efforts carried out by Architect Rodolfo Asturias through the National Council for the Protection of La Antigua Guatemala, the ruins were "rescued" and are enjoyed by the neighborhood and passersby today.

Belén School and Churches (27)
(Nuestra Señora de Belén)

Belén today is owned and administered by the religious order founded by Hermano Pedro de San José de Bethancourt (see "Historical Figures"), the Bethlemitas. It houses a school for Maya girls, a cloister for weekend spiritual retreats, and two churches.

The ruins of Belén were formerly a hospital, convent and church built by Hermano Pedro in 1666 and completed after his death in 1667. Hermano Pedro had previously been administering a hospital close to the southern boundary of San Francisco. In 1661 he received enough donations to purchase land for a building. Besides building the hospital, convent and church, he also built a kitchen and rooms to shelter travelers. It was here, also, that he established the first free school for children.

His followers, including Fray Rodrigo de la Cruz, continued his work and they were able to acquire more land and further expand between 1692 and 1705. The church was reported to be one of the most beautiful in Guatemala although the façade is very plain. Earthquake damages were reported in 1717 and again in 1751 and some reconstruction took place. The 1773 quake damaged the hospital and convent.

The first report of the building's being reused after it was abandoned was in 1852 when some Capuchin monks occupied the area. They were expelled in 1873. It was again used in 1934, this time for a sawmill. It was later rebuilt as a first class hotel administered by the nuns during the mid-20th century. The church suffered relatively little damage although work took place after 1976.

La Candelaria Church (28)
(La Candelaria)

La Candelaria ruins are a backdrop to a small park with a basketball court today. Modest repairs to limit access were carried out in the late 1990s.

Built in 1550, this hermitage serviced some 213 Maya families in a rapidly growing district in the northeast corner of town. It still held services in the Pipil language as late as 1690. Built to the east of the neighborhood's market, it was under the jurisdiction of the nearby Dominicans until 1754 when it was made a parish church. While few documents describe the history of the building, the baroque character shows that the façade was built during the 18th century and has been attributed with being perhaps one of the finest baroque examples in Santiago. Slightly damaged in 1717, it was among one of the worst hit buildings in 1773. All that remains today are the lower parts of the lace-like façade and a bit of walling on the north side. The ornate plaster decoration *(ataurique)* of shells, angels, geometric and floral patterns intermingles with various Spanish art forms.

Los Remedios Parish (29)
(Nuestra Señora de Los Remedios)

Visible from the Alameda de El Calvario, today's ruins of Los Remedios were a parish in colonial times.

Shortly after Santiago was founded, a small thatched structure was built alongside the Pensativo River. This was the first hermitage of Nuestra Señora de los Remedios. A formal tile-roofed building was later built and in 1587 a royal decree granted the hermitage financial help. Work progressed slowly as a movement began to raise the status of the hermitage to a parish church in 1594. These efforts took some fifty years to become a reality due to changes in political and ecclesiastical administration, and the church slowly fell into a state of calamity.

Historian Francisco Antonio Fuentes y Guzmán was granted a license to collect alms for rebuilding in 1679, and the church was completed eight years afterwards. It suffered damages in 1717 and 1751, and in 1762 was buried under eight feet of mud when the Pensativo River flooded the area. The church was also damaged in 1773, leaving only the façade and the walls. The Renaissance façade of Los Remedios is characteristic of the early 17th century and it is most likely that the façade was not altered after 1641. An unusually elongated church plan contains a choir bay behind the façade, a main nave and a chapel.

Santa Rosa de Lima Church (30)
(Beaterio de Santa Rosa de Lima)

Santa Rosa is one of the few monuments that are owned by a local family. It is responsible for its maintenance and carried out works in the mid-1990s. These focused on clearing a two-meter layer of debris that was causing structural damages.

Originally founded as the House of Charity (*beaterio*) of Santa Catalina de Siena, it was endowed by a noble lady with a gift of property in 1580. Membership was limited to Spanish women of the colony and, although they did not live a cloistered life, they wore white and lived as a religious community under the direction of the nearby Dominican order.

When Santa Rosa de Lima (1586–1617) became a saint, she was immediately adopted as their patron. In 1766, these nuns were granted permission to live a cloistered life, devoted to reading, sewing, spiritual exercises and the teaching of these things to a few young women entrusted in their care.

Some simple form of convent building served the community for about one hundred years prior to 1677, when it was built anew or altered and improved. The present church was begun in 1720. As one of the smaller churches in Santiago, its façade is one of the most ornate.

Santa Isabel Hermitage (31)
(Santa Isabel)

The isolated ruins of Santa Isabel are closed to the public.

The colonial neighborhood of Santa Isabel was composed of soap-makers. It was under the jurisdiction of the San Francisco Monastery until 1673. By 1690 there were some 210 Maya Kaqchikel Catholics who attended the hermitage, suggesting that a fair-sized structure must have existed. There is little information about construction or reconstruction for the hermitage, although art historians have dated it at around the second quarter of the 18th century.

All that remains today is the main façade, and parts of a wall that may have been part of the priest's house. The façade is one of the most modest in Santiago and appears to have been made by stone masons rather than architects. The area in front of the ruins, now covered with a hotel, was once the plaza for the neighborhood.

Los Dolores del Cerro Church
and Park (32)
(Nuestra Señora de los Dolores del Cerro)

A park, added in the late 1970s, is located on the property with the ruined church.

This is one of the three hermitages with the title of Our Lady of Sorrows. It was built in the northeast corner of town at the beginning of the 18th century. It housed a figure carved from one piece of cedar, found on the site, which several people had seen glowing in the dark. The chapel was enlarged in 1710 and a pilgrimage house was added. The axis of the church is centered on the Volcano Agua and does not run parallel to the axis of the walls and stairs that center on the approaching street. The level of the church entrance was about fifty feet above the level of the road, offering a beautiful view of the Valley of Panchoy.

The church was damaged in 1773 and only the main façade, main chapel and bits of the long wall stand today. Corn was farmed in the nave until the 1960s when the National Council for the Protection of La Antigua Guatemala cleaned the site in cooperation with volunteer students from the American School in Guatemala City.

A children's park was added in 1978. More efforts to preserve the area from flooding took place in the late 1990s through the National Council for the Protection of La Antigua Guatemala.

San Lázaro Cemetery Church (33)
(San Lázaro)

San Lázaro Church and grounds services the public cemetery, still in use today.

In 1634, the leper population in Santiago had grown to alarming proportions. The citizens, not wanting to mingle with lepers in the streets, demanded a place for the detention of the afflicted. Four years later, construction began on the first hospital and church in a deserted part of the city by the Guacalate, or Magdalena, River. But, due to a lack of money and poor construction, the fragile structures were damaged in 1681 and 1717. New and stronger buildings were completed in 1734 and a few years later all lepers of Santiago were ordered detained at the site by governmental decree. Despite additional damages in 1751, the hospital cared for the lepers until the abandonment of the capital after 1773.

In 1834, the property was converted to a municipal cemetery. The Cofiño family, owners of adjacent Retana Farm, donated ground for its expansion in the 20th century.

Museums

Museum of Colonial Art

(Museo de Arte Colonial – 5a Calle Oriente No. 5)
Open: Tuesdays – Fridays 9 pm to 4 pm
Weekends 9 am to noon and 2 to 4 pm
Closed holidays and Mondays.
Admission charge. Free admission Sundays.

Established in 1936–1937, this museum is located where the Old University of San Carlos de Borromeo was housed (see "University of San Carlos"). The Moorish earthquake architecture is accented by a tasteful display of magnificent religious colonial oil paintings and sculptures. Famous painters include Mexican artists, Miguel Cabrera, Juan de Correa, and Cristóbal de Villalpando and Guatemalan artist, Thomas de Merlo (1694–1739). Most of the works on display are from the 17th and 18th centuries and many are anonymous.

Guatemalan colonial sculpture was the finest in Spanish America. The museum has a number of intricately carved statues of saints, archangels and other religious figures. The figures of archangels St. Michael and St. Gabriel are on display in the graduation room, used for concerts today. These are exquisite pieces. One processional figure of Jesus of Nazareth (life-size and robed) belonged to the church of San Gaspar Vivar. The church was destroyed in 1917, the figure was brought to the museum, under progress at that time. All other sculptures are altar, or *retablo*, sculptures and were created by a workshop of artists. These had carvers, painters, some who applied the gold or silver leaf and those who gave the figure the ceramic or flesh-like look of the hands, face and legs. These are extremely expressive pieces. The display may change its location from room to room.

A graduation scene is painted on the walls in one of the old classrooms and dates from the early 1950s. It suggests a traditional Renaissance classroom and graduation scene.

Paintings by Cristóbal de Villalpando (1649?–1714), the famous Mexican artist who was contracted to create 49 paintings of the life and death of St. Francis, are the central focus in the east room. Many of this partial collection of large paintings have been restored in recent years and restoration efforts will continue until all have been "saved" from the paint falling off of the centuries-old canvasses. These are representative of the dark colonial art. One of the paintings, the baptismal scene, has the artist's self-portrait and many have the artist's signature.

Restoration work continues at this Museum. Although this government museum does not have funds for major efforts, they do have restorers on staff. Contributions come from local art lovers, including the author of this publication, and from different institutions have sponsored the restoration of different works of art. More work is needed in this area.

Casa Santo Domingo Museums

(Hotel Casa Santo Domingo Cultural Center
3a. Calle Oriente No. 28)
Open Mondays through Saturdays 9 am to 6 pm
Sundays 11:30 am to 6 pm
Closed on occasion for special activities.
Admission fee.

Located inside the Cultural Center at the Hotel Casa Santo Domingo, the Colonial Museum and the Archeological Museum are spectacular. These were founded in 1998 and offer an excellent example of Guatemalan colonial art and pre-Hispanic artifacts.

Fig. 43   St. Michael at the Colonial Art Museum
(Photo courtesy of the Museum)

Fig. 44   Restoration work at the Colonial Art Museum

Museo Colonial

The Castañeda family was able to acquire a superb collection of art over the centuries. Various churches sold pieces of art to raise funds or because art styles changed from one period to another (Baroque to Neo-classical). Indeed, many of these pieces were considered "old and worthless" just decades ago. Much of Guatemala's finest colonial art remains in private collections. This collection, however, illustrates magnificent sculptures, paintings, and silver objects.

A fascinating description is provided inside the Museo Colonial, located through the door to the north of the main altar of the church:

> "the Museum of Colonial Art is located in an area which was a communal property during the 17th and 18th centuries, and was probably used at first as a patio. This is suggested by the presence of a water reservoir. Later, it was a cemetery for children. It communicates with the High Altar through a small door. There is a large block of stone and brick that was the buttress of the east wall along the main vault. This fragment almost fell over the water reservoir. Under the huge block were found several human and animal bones, as well as small fragments of a ceramic known as *mayólica.*
>
> "The Collection exhibited here holds excellent examples of wooden sculpture, paintings and silver artifacts dating from the 16th, 17th and 18th centuries. Noteworthy is the colonial sculpture produced in the kingdom of Guatemala, which, because of its characteristics, is classified as baroque art.
>
> "Guatemala baroque sculpture flourished in the geographical region known as Audiencia de Guatemala. It had is center and enjoyed its classical period beginning in 1680, in Santiago de Guatemala, today Antigua, and extended its influence on to the late 18th century."

Museo Arqueológico

An Archeological Museum houses a small, but magnificent collection of artifacts brought from outside Antigua. (Note that the pieces found at this site during the restoration work are stored and being studied in the archeological workshop on site.) Only three jugs, or anphoras (located to right as one enters) are from the Santo Domingo site. These were used to import wine and olive oil and to export a number of agricultural products to Spain. These artifacts are some of the finest on display in the country. By placing them in a controlled climate and away from the public's touch and photographic flashes that damage these, they remain well preserved here.

A description located inside this museum reads:

> "This museum contains ceramic artifacts elaborated through different manufacturing techniques such as hollow modeling, rolling and molding, a decorated with various surface modifications.
>
> "Ceramic pieces were manufactured raw and then were fried under the sun, or fired in the open method which achieved temperatures between 700° and 900°. There is no evidence of kiln use.
>
> "The stone artifacts displayed in this museum were elaborated from raw materials transformed with stone-made tools through different methods such as wearing sown, percussion, pressure and cutting, obtaining ceremonial carved artifacts such as the mushrooms and axes.
>
> "The most important economic activity developed by the Maya was the search for and use of raw materials, as it paved the way to other activities such as the selection, extraction, transportation of these materials, as well as the manufacture of domestic and ceremonial artifacts."

Cripta de El Calvario

Also visit one of the most recent "finds" in Antigua: El Calvario crypt, or burial vault. The beautiful mural painting on stucco was discovered in September 1996. Preservation work was carried out immediately and it remains pristine. While burial vaults are located under every Catholic church and all parishoners were buried in their church, this is the finest and most decorative burial vault found to date in Antigua.

Cripta

Another crypt, or burial vault, has human remains found during the excavations of the church in the 1990s. This shows how the parishoners were buried in the churches, and monks and nuns in their convents. Later the remains were relocated in the *osario* at the end of the vault. This vault was partially rebuilt during restoration work. New work continues for our appreciation of Guatemala's past and present.

Museum of Santiago (St. James)

(Museo de Santiago –
West side of City Hall Palace)
Open: Tuesdays – Fridays 9 am to 4 pm
Weekends 9 am to 12 pm and 2 to 4 pm
Closed holidays and Mondays.
Entrance fee is charged. Free admission Sundays.

Organized by the Institute of Anthropology and History of Guatemala in 1943, it affords a variety of pre-Hispanic, colonial and post-colonial artifacts. These range from Indian bows and arrows to colonial pottery and clothes. One item of interest is Pedro de Alvarado's alleged sword although a closer view may prove this to be from a more recent era than the conquest. The sword was stolen in the 1980s and later returned to the Museum. Don Pedro's painting was created by the Guatemalan artist Humberto Garavito in the 1950s. Clothes worn by a Captain General during the 18th century show the stature of gentlemen at that time. *Macacos* (the coins made a few blocks away at the Royal Mint) are also of particular interest. A contemporary bust of the alderman and historian, Bernal Díaz del Castillo, author of the *Verdadera y Notable Relación del Descubrimiento de la Nueva España y Guatemala,* is on display in one room which also has a "special" jail cell for the more privileged. The silver altar decoration in this jail cell was probably from a local church and has been placed there for safe keeping.

The display of balls and chains found in one of the old jail cells remind us that the town prison was housed here up until the early 1950s. It is reminiscent of the days when some prisoners were tortured for their alleged crimes.

A handsome double stairway leads to the second floor. On one side of the second story is a display of interesting Maya and Spanish colonial arms. On the street side is the room where the City Council and Justice Tribune held their meetings. It was here also that prisoners were tried. City offices now occupy this room.

Old Book Museum

(Museo del Libro Antiguo – Portal del Comercio)
Open Tuesdays – Fridays 9 am to 4 pm
Weekends 9 am to 12 pm and 2 to 4 pm
Closed holidays and Mondays.
Admission fee. Free entrance Sundays.

Founded in 1956 at the location of the first printing press in colonial Guatemala, the museum displays a replica of the press transferred from Pueblo de los Angeles, Mexico in 1660. The first book, *Explicatio Apologética*, written by Bishop Payo de Rivera, was published here in Latin in 1663. The museum currently has an excellent display of rare books published during the colonial period.

Hermano Pedro Museum

(Museo del Hermano Pedro –
San Francisco Church)
Open Tuesdays – Sundays 9 am to 5 pm
Admission fee.

When Hermano Pedro de San José de Bethancourt (1626–1667) was beatified on June 22, 1980, the Franciscan order, through the efforts of Fray August Ramírez Monasterio, requested that his personal belongings be brought to Antigua. This request was made to the Archbishop's office in Guatemala City, where his belongings had remained since 1774. These personal belongings remain miraculously intact. They include his habit, hat, bedding, rosary, a skull that he used to meditate death much as St. Francis did, and his famous bell. Today these are well more than three centuries old and look exactly the way they did upon Hermano Pedro's death on April 25, 1667. It is well known that climatic characteristics in Antigua and Guatemala City are not favorable to the preservation of colonial textiles. These defy that.

This museum also displays a variety of colonial and contemporary paintings. Large colonial choir books are also of interest.

Before entering the sacristy where these items are found, one enters the magnificent vaulted chapel of San Antonio de Padua. The gilded altar with its side doorways was located to the side of the main altar in colonial times. The sculptures are exceptional. The original mural painting on the ceiling is one of the few remaining in the city. This gives the visitor an idea of what the interior of this church resembled centuries ago. A view from this area to the main cloister, now in ruins, shows us how the monastery, known as a *convento*, was quarried and cleared of debris over time.

Houses

Popenoe House
(1a Avenida Sur No. 2)

Known as "La Casa del Oidor" or "Casa del Capuchino", this fine example of Spanish colonial architecture was acquired by agricultural scientist Wilson Popenoe and his wife, Dorothy, in 1929. Extensive restoration work began by 1932 since the house was in a disastrous state of repair. While the old walls remained from the 1632 structure, roofs and floors were missing. The house, known then as a *palomar*, had been inhabited by some nine or so families.

Restoration efforts took some five years as rubble was cleaned away, cracked walls were fixed and beautifully carved wooden balconies were placed on the centuries-old windows. Wilson Popenoe, in his booklet "La Casa del Oidor" describes how few nails were found in the original structure perhaps due to the lack of iron. It was common to tie the beams together with strips of cowhide.

An excellent collection of furniture gives the house a colonial atmosphere. Some of the collection was purchased over the years from the highlands while another part of the collection was brought from Honduras in the 1930s when the Popenoes decorated the house.

This house's history began when Don Luis de las Infantas Mendoza arrived in Guatemala in the early 1630s as the Chief Justice or President of the Court (Oidor de la Real Audiencia) for the region that extended from Chiapas, Mexico to Costa Rica. Accompanied by his wife, Feliciana de Hermosilla and six servants, they built the house in a Moorish architectural style. Don Luis later had house arrest due to allegations of bribery. It was from this house that he could go directly to the Palace of the Captains General and return home. In 1640 he was transferred to Mexico to another position.

Little is known about the house throughout the 18th century. We do know that it was auctioned off by two elderly women in 1738 to cover a mortgage or donation of 400 pesos owned to Santo Domingo Church and Monastery. Diego Guerra, Chief Royal Horseman, purchased the colonial home. We may also assume that it suffered damages in the 1717, 1751 and 1773 earthquakes and subsequent changes by different owners. The Popenoes purchased the house in 1929 from Ciriaco Peralta and it was declared as "almost a complete ruin". Roof damage was registered in 1976 due to the earthquake.

The main entrance reflects 17th century architecture with very high walls and a Moorish stone-arched entrance (*zaguán*). Door-knockers are placed up high so horsemen would not have to dismount upon arrival during colonial times although the door dates from the 1930s. Corridors with gargoyles enclose a beautiful garden with the area for stables off to the south and two large living rooms around the patio. A small library was partially restored as was the dining room but part of the house has been left in ruins in memory of the earthquakes that destroyed Antigua for so many years.

While the living room seems somewhat dark today, it reflects colonial life and houses a fine collection of paintings and furniture. Originals and copies of colonial art depict the main historical figures from Guatemala: Don Pedro de Alvarado, Bishop Francisco Marroquín and Hermano Pedro just to mention a few. Windows with traditional brick bench alcoves allowed ladies to enjoy the street view from inside. Shutters (no glass) are adjusted for a balance of privacy and light.

A small library adjacent to the main living room was restored by the Popenoes and still provides a reading room for family members. It is quite possible that the fireplace here was the first to be added in Antigua since braziers were used in colonial times. Fire-

Fig. 45   Casa Popenoe doorway

Fig. 46   Casa Popenoe door knocker

places were added in the 20ᵗʰ century. While museum-like today, it is used by the Popenoe daughters. Marion, a serious archeologist, claims that a ghost or spirit of sorts haunts the house. Many, in fact, claim that there are still spirits behind the walls of Antigua but it seems that they only appear "after dark". A photograph of her father is on the table. Only a few of his diplomas and awards are in his old master bedroom.

Wilson Popenoe is well known for his work on introducing the avocado to California, co-founding the Zamorano Institute in Honduras, and much more. In the main plaza of the city, the following plaque was placed:

Presented by

CALIFORNIA AVOCADO SOCIETY

1946

in recognition and appreciation of the great contributions
of Antigua, and of all Guatemala to the development
of the avocado industry in California.

A healthy, growing child salutes a generous parent.

A favorite part of the house for most is the service area with its kitchen, bath, *pila*, messenger pigeon cove and a spice garden with built up beds (*arriates*). All this reflects the tranquility of colonial times. Four centuries of hearth smoke blackens the walls of the *chimenea*. Used up until the 1970s, when a modern kitchen was added, this *chimenea* is still used for cooking traditional meals today. Ceramic pipes are hidden in the raised hearth; while one cooked, water was heated for the nearby hot water baths. Indeed, the baths are a brilliant example of a 1632 jacuzzi! Most of the ceramic collection reflects the 1930s work done by the Montiel family in Antigua. Other ceramic pieces were brought from other countries.

A small stairway takes us through a fascinating pigeon cove (*palomar*) with three walls of private *casitas* for the colonial (messenger) pigeon mail service up to a fabulous view from the roof. San Francisco Church dominates the view to the south as the Volcano Agua and the entire city blends with the coffee plantations, mountains and volcanoes.

Doña Luisa's House
(4a Calle Oriente No. 12)

Occupied today by Doña Luisa Xicotencatl restaurant and bakery, this house was originally purchased by the nuns from La Concepción Convent in 1650 for 400 pesos. Today it is one third of its original size.

Santiago provided a number of distinguished residents. These included two magistrates of Antigua (1672, 1765), the General of the Troops of the Cavalry battalion (1677), two priests (one of whom was the Master of Ceremonies and Chaplain of the Choir of the Cathedral, 1686–1696), the Captain of the Militia (1715), Antonio Ortiz Urruela and many others of particular interest. A list of previous residents is located on an information area inside the restaurant.

Two stories provided commercial and residential areas in colonial times: the first floor for two shops, offices and services; the second for a living area, bedrooms, dining room, kitchen and wash area (*pila*). A carriage and horses entered through the large entryway (*zaguán*). Leaving the carriage there the horses made their way through the horse-size walkway to the stables in the back. A large *pila*, kitchen area and water tanks provide a typical service area in the second patio with an access to the second story. The second floor may also be reached from the first courtyard up a beautiful stone stairway to the old living room that provides a spectacular view of the volcanoes and backside of the Cathedral.

When Antigua was on the verge of "coming to life" at the end of the 1960s, this house was on the market for US$30,000. Deemed "too expensive" by many who saw that to restore it would cost "a fortune", little necessary work was carried out by the new owners in the early 1970s. Earthquake damage did not escape this colonial gem when the second floor façade crashed into the street below around noon on February 6th, 1976. Restoration work carried out by the most recent owners, The Wheeler family, began around 1987. Leather ties on the second story roof, dating back to previous centuries, were found. It appears that iron nails were too expensive and leather proved to be earthquake proof due to its flexibility. Other artifacts were also discovered during this major restoration effort. A visit to the restaurant opens this house up for us today. The name Doña Luisa Xicotencatl refers to the Pedro de Alvarado's "faithful companion", a Tlaxcaltec princess he was awarded in Mexico. She may have lived in a house down the street from the restaurant today.

Casa de los Leones –
House of the Lions
(5a Avenida Norte No. 17)

Two rampant stone lions and an assortment of stone door frames decorate the entrance of the House of the Lions that houses the Hotel Posada de Don Rodrigo today. This magnificent colonial house has a typical *zaguán*, main courtyard and back patio with a *pila*. Photographs from the 1940s show truly no change at all in the front courtyard to the present. A restaurant was located in the stable area in the 1960s.

Foundation fragments may date back to the 16th century when this property was awarded to a Spanish family but probably no construction has survived from that time. The house we see today reflects "earthquake architecture" from the late 17th and 18th centuries due to the short squat walls that may have been higher in the 17th century. It was quite common to lower the height of walls after the 1717 and 1751 earthquakes. The living room area also shows how the walls were "cut" to show a buttress-like effect when, in fact, the thicker upper walls may have been "provisional" with the pole-earth (*bajareque*) walls. These have outlived their provisional character.

Built with massive walls and a typical distribution of rooms around the central courtyard, there is also a magnificent kitchen, service area and remains of the stables built around the back courtyard. Colonial doors are unique and have shutters to adapt to just the right amount of light and air desired in each room. An unusual corner window was restored after one of the many earthquakes. Very few houses in Antigua have corner windows. Special permission was required for this.

The house preserves its exquisite colonial atmosphere characteristic of the colonial era. Restored in 1968-71 by Carlos and Isabel Dorión, the adjacent house was adjoined to create the hotel. Today the Posada is one of the most beautiful and traditional houses in Antigua. Owner Jaroslav Chour and his family have added a very special touch.

Casa del Conde
(Portal de las Panaderas No. 9)

Located across from the Cathedral on the main square, this house must have been much larger in colonial times. Its walls are built with solid earthquake architecture from the 18th century. The first house on this site, occupied today by shops and the Restaurant Café Condesa, reflects much of what its menu tells us today:

> "... this beautiful colonial house was built in 1549; it later became part of the Royal Houses in the country's capital city, Santiago de Guatemala. The first Count to occupy the house (1609) was the Count of Gomera who served as President of

the Court, Captain General and Governor from 1609-1623, and was the first "cloak and dagger" president (non-educated) who had no vote within his own court. Successive Counts inherited the title and occupied the house for many years until the capital city was transferred in 1775, to modern Guatemala City.

"Like many old houses, this house has its bits of folklore. Supposedly, one of the counts made an unexpected return from a voyage and found his wife in an indiscretion with the butler. Rumor has it that the butler was buried alive by the angry Count. During reparations after the 1976 earthquake, the rumor was supported when a skeleton was discovered within the pantry wall... and apparently had been buried standing up!

"Just to be on the safe side, the house was exorcised in 1992. And since the Café has been established, no strange noises have been heard..."

The house is well preserved with its back patio, *pila* and colonial kitchen. A wall-fountain, *búcaro*, highlights the front patio.

Landívar House
(Calle del Cementerio No. 40)

The great colonial poet, Rafael Landívar, was born here on October 27, 1731. He studied at the Jesuit school at the Compañía de Jesús in Antigua, Colegio de San Francisco de Borja. He is best known for his work, *Rusticatio Mexicana*, dedicated to the city of Santiago.

Very little of his house is left and most of it is in a bad state of repair. A vaulted room with its gargoyles and traditional masonry construction are of interest. It appears that these walls are originally from the 17th or 18th centuries. A typical kitchen with its *chimenea* is located at the back of the property. The Municipality of Antigua is in charge of this, semi-abandoned property.

The Monument of Rafael Landívar, with the poet's remains, was built next door in 1953. Located on the Alameda de Santa Lucía, it resembles the old University of San Carlos with its Moorish architecture.

Fiestas and Holidays

Fiestas and Holidays

Fiestas and holidays in Antigua vary in size, elaborateness, mood, and tradition and remain as the main cultural current in Antigua. Only the celebrants' passion and complete enjoyment of the occasion transcend the many differences. In most instances, vendors from neighboring villages erect stalls in front of the old churches and sell everything from excellent local foods to helium balloons. *Fiestas* are mostly of religious character but may also include beauty contests, sports events, carnivals, and parades. Rarely is a *fiesta* limited to one day. On many occasions, *gigantes* and *cabezones* dance in the streets to marimba the day before the main celebration. A few of the larger and more unusual events are detailed below preceded by a calendar of festivities and national holidays. All dates listed in the calendar represent a unique and colorful celebration and every effort should be made to not only watch the spectacle but to assimilate the diverse cultural energies as well. The most significant and spectacular celebrations remain religious in character: the highlight of these is Lent and Holy Week.

Calendar of Holidays

* National holiday

January 1*	**New Year's Day**
Moveable	**Carnival (Mardi Gras)**

Carnival is a small celebration with some festivities in schools. The traditional *cascarones*, made of eggshells filled with colorful confetti, are broken on friends' heads.

139

Moveable*	First Friday of Lent

Lent begins with Ash Wednesday. This is a holiday for some in Antigua, including those processional carriers and City Hall employees have a holiday on the first Friday of Lent.

Moveable*	Holy Wednesday (noon)
	Maundy Thursday
	Good Friday
	Saturday before Easter
	Easter Sunday

Holy Week (*Semana Santa*) is by far the largest and most spectacular holiday of the year. The thousands of participants dressed in Roman costumes and the tens of thousands of visitors and *peregrinos* (pilgrims) combine to produce a massive spectacle that remains unparalleled in this hemisphere. The entire week becomes a living theater of Christ's passion and death. Holy Week starts on Palm Sunday and ends on Easter Sunday. The dates change every year and are determined by the first full moon of spring. The first Sunday after the full moon is Easter. For a complete schedule of Lent and Holy Week, consult the publication, *Lent and Holy Week in Antigua*, by the author. There are more than 50 activities: *velaciones* (holy vigils), processions, and carpet making.

May 1*	International Labor Day
May 10	Mother's Day

Special activities, called *actos,* take place at schools where mothers are graced with school project gifts made especially for them; always a holiday for mothers.

Fig. 47   Carpet making with flowers and sawdust

Fig. 48   Holy Week

Fig. 49 Carpets for Holy Week

Fig. 50   Good Friday

Moveable **Corpus Christi**

Corpus Christi is a major celebration with a small procession that leaves each church, processing around the neighborhood and returning to the church where the holy sacrament remains on display for a traditional nine days. The flute and drum players in front of the church indicate a celebration and attract visitors. The first Corpus Christi is celebrated at San José Catedral and the other active churches in Antigua on following Sundays. Other surrounding towns and villages celebrate this occasion after that date. There is usually a nice fair in front of the church with a delicious variety of foods, cotton candy and goodies. This celebration was very important in the 16th century when the Spanish tried to attract the reluctant Indian population inside the church.

June 17 **Father's Day (holiday)**
June 30* **Army Day (1871 Revolution)**
July 25* **St. James Day**

This is to celebrate St. James Day, (Santiago) who remains the patron saint of Antigua. While the main celebration is July 25th, the entire month is filled with cultural activities, sponsored by various cultural organizations. City Hall coordinates this magnificent display of arts, sports competitions, beauty contests, oratory competitions, and others. Programs are available at the beginning of the month on the second floor of the Palace of City Hall. *Toritos* (men with bull-like frames carrying fireworks on their backs) dance through the square on the evenings of July 24th and 25th, accompanied by firecrackers, *bombas* and music.

September 15* **Independence Day**

Characterized by parades and marathons with runners that carry torches from one town to another, this holiday is also celebrated with school contests and much more. September 15 commemorates Guatemala's independence from Spain in 1821. It was after this that the various provinces of Guatemala formed the Confederation of Central American Provinces and, later, formed the different republics more or less as we know them today.

October 12   **Columbus Day / Día de la Raza**

Known as *Día de la Raza* (Day of the Race), this is not a national holiday but is usually observed as a bank holiday. As a time of reflection of the Spanish arrival in Guatemala in 1524 and how that has influenced the Maya culture over the past five centuries, cultural groups prepare a variety of activities.

October 20*   **Revolution Day**

Commemoration of the 1944 Revolution is a reflection of the social reforms carried out at that time. These encompassed abolishing a number of taxes, including the colonial labor tax, and establishing institutions such as the Instituto Guatemalteco de Seguridad Social (IGSS).

November 1*   **All Saints' Day**

A national holiday brings families together with the traditional meal known as *fiambre*. This mixture of cold cooked vegetables, meats, fishes and cheeses is prepared by family members and enjoyed at lunchtime. It is said that the first *fiambre* was created when a number of families gathered at a cemetery to visit their deceased family members. While joining in a picnic lunch, a gust of wind lifted up the tablecloth and mixed all the foods. From then on, family members take their *fiambre* to cemeteries to visit their deceased loved ones. While *fiambre* in Antigua is enjoyed at home, a trip to the cemetery is in order, usually on the following day, November 2nd, which is All Souls' Day, or the Day of the Dead.

December 7
at 6 PM   Burn the Devil

Antigüeños take part in the tradition of lighting small fires made with old papers and small branches, and burning firecrackers in front of their homes. The most elaborate celebration is around the fountain of La Concepción where an effigy of a large devil is lit in flames. In the 1980s, the families of the neighborhood, or *barrio*, joined to create a wonderful week long festival including concerts on a small stage built for the occasion and a food festival.

December 15   Posadas begin

Posadas leave each active Catholic church to stay at a nearby house. Those who accompany the cart carrying figures of Joseph and Mary are first refused entry, just as Joseph and Mary were, but after repeated requests the *posada* is allowed entry to the house. Traditional posadas songs enhance the air. A celebration is waiting for them, with traditional Christmas *ponche* and *tamales*. The *posada* stays the night and continues on its journey the following evening to another house where the scenario is repeated. While the *posadas* process from one house to another, the carriers use beautiful candle-lit lanterns and a large supply of firecrackers and the more aggressive *canchinflines* to announce their journey.

As Christmas gets closer, families and church members create nativity scenes known as *nacimientos* in churches and homes. Made with dyed sawdust, colored paper, clay or elaborately carved wooden images, great detail goes into creating these traditional scenes. All nacimientos are accented with local touches of Guatemalan folklore. Completed by midnight on Christmas Eve, some of the more elaborate church *nacimientos* are found inside San

Francisco Church and the Cathedral where children participate actively and the Obras Sociales del Hermano Pedro inside the hospital.

December 24*   Christmas Eve

At 3:00 pm, *Gigantes* leave Escuela de Cristo Church and dance around the main streets of Antigua accompanied by a marimba band. This is to announce the procession of the Virgin of O on Christmas Day. Preparations for the midnight celebrations include exchanging wrapped gifts, cards and preparing for a nice midnight dinner with a turkey or ham feast or a more humble *ponche* and *tamal* meal. The importance here is the family, not necessarily all the material items that appear on the scene. Churchgoers attend mass or other Christmas services. Everyone waits in anticipation for midnight when there is a crescendo of fireworks, firecrackers, hugs, and prayer as the figure of baby Jesus is added to the *nacimiento*, accompanied by the tune played on the turtle shell. Presents are opened and then families enjoy Christmas dinner.

December 25*   Christmas Day

A somewhat subdued day, families join with hugs at noon and firecrackers are heard.

December 28   All Fools' Day

Known as *Día de los Inocentes*, many play silly jokes.

December 31*   New Year's Eve

Celebrated as in many other countries, families and friends participate in welcoming the New Year and giving thanks for those blessings received. New Year resolutions are also common!

Physical Environment

Physical Environment

Antigua, with an altitude of 5,049 feet, is designated as *tierra templada* and has only two seasons. The dry season, or *verano* (summer) lasts from November through mid-May with daytime temperatures of 75° to 80° F and nighttime temperatures of 40° to 50° F. The remainder of the year is the wet season, or *invierno* (winter), with daytime temperatures of 65° to 70° F. Rainfall is between 30 and 50 inches annually.

The colonial capital is located in a highland valley encompassed by three volcanoes: Agua (12,307 feet), Fuego (12,579 feet) and Acatenango (13,000 feet). Only Fuego is active. The valley floor is an ash-filled basin. Rich volcanic soil produces some of the finest coffee in the world. The valley may have contained a lake at one time as the old name Panchoy (Valley of the Lake) suggests. While there is no historical evidence, archaeologists and geologists agree on this. The valley is covered by expanses of silk oak and pine forests though portions have been cleared for agricultural purposes.

Hill of the Cross
(Cerro de la Cruz)

Cerro de la Cruz offers a panoramic view of the entire valley. Since this area does not have proper security, it is recommended to drive up and/or take an escort. Contact the local Municipal Tourism Police on the side of the City Hall Palace to check on daily times that they may escort you safely. You may also drive north on First Avenue and follow it up to the hill, where you will see a bronze sculpture of the patron saint, Saint James given to the city of Antigua by the Spanish government in 1969. The cross itself, located farther down the hill, was erected in the 1930s with the efforts of Mayor Guillermo Arzú Matheu. It fell down during the 1976 earthquake and was immediately re-erected. In 2001, an Association composed of a small group of people interested in establishing a park was created. Members include city council members to ensure the first steps in setting up a municipal park.

Volcanoes

Guatemala contains more volcanoes per square mile than any other country in the world. Reaching heights of 14,000 feet, the massive cones present the opportunity for some of the most spectacular and exciting hikes available. Three of Guatemala's larger volcanoes are located within a few miles of Antigua.

Volcano Agua
12,307 FT. (3,752 meters)

Of the three volcanoes, Agua is the easiest to climb. The ascent begins from Santa María de Jesús. A shelter is located in the crater and can be used for resting. Buses to Santa María can be found at the Antigua market. The climb takes about six hours and taking a guide is recommended. As of this date, trails are not marked and it is easy to get lost along the way.

Volcano Acatenango
13,000 FT. (3,960 meters)

The ascent starts 0.3 Km. before the Acatenango Junction. It is always recommended taking a local experienced guide on volcano climbs. The summit can become extremely cold at night with sudden winds of up to 100 MPH. This climb is the most difficult of those in the area.

Volcano Fuego
12,579 FT. (3,835 meters)

The route should not be attempted by the inexperienced and under no circumstances alone. The summit of Fuego is inaccessible on some days due to its activity. This volcano began a moderate eruption in 2002 and is quite beautiful at night.

Surrounding Towns and Areas

When the Spaniards first arrived in Santiago, the only signs of inhabitants were the remains of a small Maya community on the slopes of the Volcano Agua that had been abandoned for several years and, perhaps, some dispersed farmers. It was not until after the distribution of conquered lands that we find the humble origins of the many surrounding communities. As lands were granted to the Spaniards around the capital site, a need for agricultural labor became apparent. This necessity was taken care of for the most part by raids. Spanish captains accompanied by ten or twelve of their soldiers led by good guides would attack settlements of still unconquered Mayas and carry off six to ten captives. Taken back to the *milpas*, the Mayas would be put to work under threat of death. These raids, repeated many times, resulted in the population increase of several hundreds per *milpa*. The general definition of *milpa* is "corn field" but Christopher Lutz specifically defines *milpa* as an agricultural community. Not all of the villages had such brutal origins. In many instances milpas were populated by Mayas previously employed in the conquest or were brought from other regions because of a particularly useful trade. The common denominator, however, was the forced transplant of the Maya populations to work on Spanish-owned land. The Maya slaves, however, were emancipated in 1542 with the Laws of Burgos and some were awarded lands of their own, particularly Alvarado's warriors. Though they worked as freemen, they were usually burdened with heavy tributes. Through the centuries, shops, businesses and city governments were established and the present-day communities evolved. While many Spanish-owned *milpas* developed into permanent Maya and mestizo communities, several did not experience the same population growth. Lutz attributes this in part to infertility of the soil or poor water resources, the failure of Spanish owners to populate their *milpas* with Mayas, or the Mayas' inability to survive the severe epidemics that plagued indigenous populations during the 17th century. Today some of the villages maintain a life style that has changed very little since the colonial period.

Ciudad Vieja

5 Km. from Antigua
Altitude: 5,012 feet
Fiesta: December 8

A historical account of the founding and subsequent destruction of the second capital is described in the first chapter of this publication. Past writers have placed the exact site of the second colonial capital in Ciudad Vieja proper. But archeological works carried out in the 1940s have proven that the former capital was actually located in San Miguel Escobar (to the east of Ciudad Vieja). Ciudad Vieja received the survivors from the flood. During the colonial period, Ciudad Vieja was a suburb, populated by Mexican Tlaxcaltecs. Guatemalan Mayas populated San Miguel Escobar. The ruins located to the south of the square, once thought to be portions of Doña Beatriz's Palace, are veritably the remains of an 18th century structure. The church, labeled the "first Cathedral" was, in fact, a Franciscan church and monastery built by Architect Diego de Porres in the 18th century. Ironically, San Miguel Escobar appears as a suburb of Ciudad Vieja today.

The fiesta for the *Virgen de la Concepción* on December 8th is one of the most colorful in the valley. Celebrations begin the day before with the Burning of the Devil and folkloric dances are the focal point after mass on the 8th. Dances include "The Seven Virtues and Seven Vices" and more. The largest fireworks display, including *granadas*, is lit at this time.

Jocotenango

Northwest of Antigua
Altitude: 5,082 feet
Fiesta: August 15

Today Jocotenango has a magnificent procession within the Lent celebrations and its patron fiesta on August 15th and is a city that has grown recently.

At the time of Pedro de Alvarado's death, a great portion of the lands in the Jocotenango valley was in his name. Bishop Francisco Marroquín arranged for the development of these lands by transplanting gold miners from different regions. After the emancipation of the Mayas in 1542, they applied for and received land titles in the area. In 1602, royal permission was given to the Dominican order to found a vicarage in the town. A small chapel was built which possibly still stands as the northern portion of a larger baroque church added during the latter part of the 17th century. The fountain in front of the church was placed in public service on June 30, 1773. The church was severely damaged during the 1773 earthquake and renovated some fifty years later. During the colonial period, Jocotenango served as a gateway to the capital. It was here that church authorities and government officials greeted distinguished visitors from Mexico and Spain and escorted them into the city with great ceremony.

San Antonio Aguas Calientes

8 Km. from Antigua
Altitude: 5,115 feet
Fiesta: January 20

San Antonio is a typical Maya village in the Antigua area. Predominately an agricultural community, it was founded on the lands of Juan de Chávez around 1530.

The town's proximity to Antigua and the rise in tourism have contributed to an increase in weaving and textile shops located along the road into the city. Though many of the items are brought to the shops from other regions, much of the weaving is done in San Antonio. The local Maya blouses (*huipiles*) are among the finest in the country, both for technique and color combination. Intense bargaining over prices is traditional.

San Felipe de Jesús

2 Km. from Antigua
Altitude: 5,150 feet
Fiestas: April 30 and May 1

San Felipe is the site of annual pilgrimages on the first Friday of Lent and during Holy Week. A carved wooden figure of Jesus is worshiped by the faithful from all over the country. It is said that the faithful have been praying to it since 1620. It was first in the church of San Juan Perdido in Los Tarros Farm, San Lucas Cotzumalguapa. When the farm was invaded by bats, neighbors brought the sculpture to Santiago. Then, in 1819, Father don Manuel Francisco Barrutia had a small church built for the sculpture with materials from the ruined monastery of La Merced in Antigua. It appears in the famous Good Friday procession since 1820.

Gaspar Arias Dávila founded San Felipe in the early 1540s. Its sharp gothic style façade contrasts the colonial architecture of the rest of the Antigua area. The main nave was demolished after the 1976 earthquake and the church was rebuilt in the 1980s.

An excellent silver factory is located two blocks from the main square and visitors are welcome to watch the craftsmen at work. Typical and ceramic shops are scattered throughout the town and local restaurants serve excellent Guatemalan meals, *comidas típicas,* including *pepián.*

Santa María de Jesús

9 Km. from Antigua
Altitude: 6,765 feet
Fiesta: January 2

Two thousand feet above Antigua on the upper slopes of the Volcano Agua, Santa María de Jesús is the highest city in the area. While the road dates from colonial times, it was paved in 1998, making the town much more accessible. Santa María de Jesús is the starting point for the climb up the Volcano Agua.

It was founded in the latter part of the 16th century and populated with Mayas transplanted from another region, probably Quetzaltenango. Its population was charged with providing Santiago with lumber from the surrounding forests. In recognition of their forced labors, the town was first given the name *Aserradero* (lumberyard). Eventually the village was emancipated and evolved into an agricultural community. Plots with corn and vegetables now cover the steep sides of the volcano. In colonial times, it is recorded that this village supplied ice from the crater of Volcano Agua for the Crown in Santiago, which maintained a monopoly of it. Ice was served with the drinks provided at the inauguration of the Cathedral in 1680.

All Kaqchikel women and most of the older men wear traditional dress. Weaving remains a highly regarded craft.

A colorful celebration, *El Dulce Nombre* (the sweet name), is held on January 2nd, with firecrackers, rockets, food shops, processions, and music in the Central Plaza. The celebration generally lasts for a few days. Corpus Christi is traditionally celebrated with a similar passion. That date is moveable.

Historical Figures

Pedro de Alvarado (1485–1541)

This ruthless adventurer helped Hernán Cortés subdue the Aztecs in Mexico and conquered Guatemala with a small army. Born in Badajoz, Spain, Alvarado went to the West Indies in 1510. He joined the expedition of Diego Velásquez to Cuba in 1511 and received a grant of land there. Alvarado accompanied Cortés to Mexico in 1519 and continued on to Guatemala in 1521. In 1524, he succeeded in seizing Guatemala with the help of Maya allies. He then became the Captain General of colonial Guatemala. Alvarado died in Guadalajara, Mexico days before the destruction of the capital of Santiago de Guatemala, located on the slopes of the Volcano Agua (Valley of Almolonga).

Leonor de Alvarado Xicotencatl (1524–1583)

Doña Leonor, the illegitimate daughter of Pedro de Alvarado and the Tlaxcaltec princess, Doña Luisa Xicotencatl, was the first *mestiza* (half-Spanish and half-Maya) in Guatemala. Her palace was located on the Calle de La Concepción (now 4a Calle Oriente).

Pedro de San José de Bethancourt (1626–1667)

Hermano Pedro will be canonized on July 31, 2002 and Guatemalans venerate him more than any other local religious figure. Born in the Canary Islands, he embarked for Cuba to see the New World. He arrived in Santiago de Guatemala and attended the Franciscan School but gave up in despair after three years. Upon

161

returning to the village of Petapa, he confided his tragic failure to the Virgin Mary at the church. It is told that he received encouragement from her lips and thus returned to the capital. He was readmitted to the convent and became inspired to help the sick. For a few pesos, he purchased land, erecting a small thatched hut where he set up his first hospital for the poor. He soon received funds to found the Hospital of Belén. His tomb, now a shrine, is in San Francisco Church, where many go to ask him for favors or blessings. He also founded a religious order. The Bethlemitas are active today at the Convent of Belén. Hermano Pedro was beatified in 1980.

Bernal Díaz del Castillo (1495–1585)

This famous soldier and historian came to the New World to find adventure, fame and fortune. He fought no fewer than 119 battles (his own tally) under such men as Cortés and Alvarado in Panama, Mexico and colonial Guatemala. Fortune he never won, but the devotion of his contemporaries and fame he gained beyond his dreams. After settling in Santiago, where he was a permanent alderman of the City Council, he became frustrated by the inaccurate histories of the conquest and wrote his own version: *True History of the Conquest of New Spain and Guatemala* (1568). The original of this document may be seen at the National Archives in Guatemala City.

Beatriz de la Cueva (1519–1541)

Doña Beatriz, the daughter of the Duke of Albuquerque (Prime Minister of Spain), married Pedro de Alvarado and succeeded him as head of the government. The first woman governor in the Americas, her forty-hour reign ended when the capital flooded and she and her daughter died. It is believed that she was buried in the crypt under the main altar of the Cathedral (see Cathedral) but these remains were unearthed in 1943–1944 and later lost.

Rafael Landívar (1731–1793)

One of Guatemala's most renowned poets, he was educated at the Jesuit School at La Compañía de Jesús but was expelled with the Jesuits in 1767. Although he died in Italy, his tomb and monument are located on the Alameda of Santa Lucía and his home, now in ruins, is found just behind the monument.

Francisco Marroquín (1500–1563)

This remarkable man came to Guatemala with Pedro de Alvarado in 1530 and introduced Christianity to the Mayas along with instilling Christian ways among the colonists. Upon Doña Beatriz's death in 1541, he assumed the role of temporary head of the government and helped in relocating the destroyed capital. Marroquín was the first bishop in Guatemala. He oversaw the construction of the Cathedral and Archbishop's Palace. He is also accredited with founding the first school in colonial Guatemala in 1532. He spent his last years in the palace that he had built in San Juan del Obispo.

Diego de Porres (1677–1714)

Porres was the major architect in Santiago during a time of urban development between the earthquake of 1717 and his death in 1741. While it is difficult to enumerate all his works, some of the monumental structures that he designed and built are: Escuela de Cristo, Santa Clara, the Royal Mint, Capuchinas, Escuela de Cristo, and

City Hall. He also took part in the design and construction of the churches at Ciudad Vieja, Esquipulas, and Granada (Nicaragua). Porres displayed his abilities as a hydraulic engineer in Capuchinas and the fountain of the Central Plaza.

Cristóbal de Villalpando (1639–1714)

The renowned painter, Villalpando, was born in Mexico and moved to Santiago. While living with the Franciscan brothers, he created a series of 49 large oil paintings depicting the life and death of San Francisco de Asis. Some of these may be viewed at the Museum of Colonial Art and San Francisco Church.

Earthquakes

Chronological Record of Damaging Earthquakes 1526–1998

1526 July 19 or 20 – Damaging earthquake that caused removal of Spanish settlement to Ciudad Vieja.

1541 September 10 – Two destructive earthquakes killed approximately 150 Spaniards and at least 600 Indians and Blacks. Two days of rains prior to the earthquakes added damage from avalanches and landslides. The primary Spanish settlement then moved to Santiago (present-day Antigua).

1565 February – Series of violent earthquakes caused extensive damage in and near Santiago.

1575 – Several large shocks caused damage in San Salvador and also in Santiago de Guatemala.

1577 November 30 – Earthquake swarm. Largest shock caused much damage in Santiago.

1586 December 23 – Long earthquake sequence beginning **January 16, 1585**, and ending with largest shock on above date. Accompanied by eruption of Volcano Fuego. Santiago was destroyed, causing many deaths.

1607 April – Many buildings collapsed, killing a number of people in Santiago.

1651 February 18 – Extensive damage in Santiago.

1681 July 22 – A swarm of earthquakes caused extensive damage in Santiago.

1684 August – Earthquake swarm caused extensive damage and loss of life in Santiago area; stronger than 1651 shock.

1702 August 4 – A strong earthquake caused extensive damage in Santiago.

1717 September 29, 30 – Santiago damaged on September 29, destroyed the following day; loss of life was extensive; large aftershock on **October 3**. Earthquakes accompanied by violent eruptions of Fuego.

1751 March 4 – Santiago damaged. Cathedral dome destroyed.

1765 April 20 – Fifty killed and many injured; many towns destroyed in the Department of Chiquimula. Earthquake may have originated on the Motagua fault.

1765 October – The earthquake of "San Rafael" severely damaged many towns in Guatemala.

1773 July 29 – This major event was part of an earthquake swarm beginning in May and continuing until December. Very strong shocks occurred on **June 11**. Large aftershocks occurred on **September 7** and **December 14**. Santiago was completely destroyed, and many deaths resulted. The capital was then moved to Guatemala City. These earthquakes were felt even more strongly in Chimaltenango and Quetzaltenango, nearer to the Motagua fault, and thus the Motagua fault may have been the source of these earthquakes.

1830 April 1 – A swarm, similar to that of 1773, destroyed many buildings in Antigua. Major aftershocks on **April 23**.

1852 May 16 – Damage in the vicinity of Quetzaltenango.

1853 February 9 – Major earthquake caused great alarm in Quetzaltenango. Also strongly felt in Antigua and Amatitlán.

1855 January 1-26 – Swarm with main events on the 18th and 26th. Damage at Cantel and Zunil.

1859 December 8 – Major earthquake near El Salvador-Guatemala border. Houses were shattered in Escuintla and Amatitlán.

1860 December 19 – Extensive damage to churches and homes in Escuintla. Aftershocks continued until **December 31**.

1861 August 27 – Damage to homes and churches in Conguaco and Jalpatagua.

1862 December 19 – Antigua, Amatitlán, Escuintla, Tecpán, and neighboring areas were severely damaged. Damage to many churches and ancient constructions. Slight damage to old churches in Guatemala City; astronomical observatory reported tilt of 3'29".

1863 December 12 – The earthquake centered near Guatemala City, caused change in flow of springs in the northern part of the city, and earth fractures opened in the areas of Jocotenango and El Bosque, causing panic throughout the city.

1870 June 12 – Extensive damage in the regions of Chiquimulilla, Cuilapa and Ixhuatán. A later quake caused serious damage in Cuilapa. Aftershocks continued until the **23rd**.

1874 September 3 (or possibly 18) – Antigua, Chimaltenango and Patzicía were damaged and 200 people killed.

1881 August 13 – Earthquake swarm felt in San Marcos – possible damage in Chinique.

1885 November 22 – Strong shocks; damage in Amatitlán.

1885 December 18 – Amatitlán destroyed. Cracking of ground; new hot springs on shores of Amatitlán. Many shocks into **January 1886**. Volcano Pacaya increased level of activity.

168

1902 April 19 – Destroyed the city of Quetzaltenango. Extensive loss of life. Activity continued until **September 23**, when an earthquake was strongly felt and an eruption of Volcano Santa María began. (Magnitude 8.3)

1912 June 12 – (Magnitude 6.8)

1913 March 9 – Strong earthquake, felt in the central region of Santa Rosa and also in the Departments of Cuilapa and Santa Rosa de Lima. Felt over large parts of the country. Many deaths and much destruction.

1915 September 7 – Heavy damage in Jutiapa. Felt strongly over large areas of Guatemala and El Salvador. (Magnitude 7.9)

1917 December 25 – A series of earthquakes that began on **November 17, 1917**, and continued into **January 1918. December 25** main event had magnitude of 6 plus and maximum Modified Mercalli intensity of VIII-IX. In Guatemala City, cracks opened the streets, and about 40 percent of the houses were destroyed or seriously damaged. The Colon Theatre collapsed while filled with people; school buildings, churches, asylums, hospitals, sugar mills, the post office, the railway station, and the British and American legation buildings were thrown down, and many occupants were killed or injured. Later another destructive earthquake of this series was the **January 3, 1918**, earthquake.

INSTRUMENTAL DATA (RICHTER SCALE) Only those registering 6.0 or above on the Richter Scale appear in this list.

Date	Location N. Lat.	W. Long.	Magnitude
17 Apr 1919	14.50	-91.75	7.0
04 Feb 1921	15.00	-91.00	7.5
26 Sep 1931	14.50	-91.50	6.2
22 May 1932	14.25	-90.00	6.0
19 May 1934	14.75	-91.25	6.2
20 Jan 1939	13.50	-91.50	6.5
28 Sep 1939	15.50	-91.50	6.2
05 Dec 1939	14.50	-91.50	6.7
27 July 1940	14.25	-91.50	6.7
11 Apr 1942	14.75	-91.50	6.5
06 Aug 1942	14.00	-91.00	8.3
08 Aug 1942	14.25	-91.50	6.5
31 Aug 1943	14.25	-91.50	6.7
23 Sep 1943	15.00	-91.50	6.7
02 Oct 1944	14.50	-89.75	6.5
27 Oct 1945	15.00	-91.25	6.7
05 Jan 1946	15.00	-91.00	6.0
26 June 1946	14.75	-90.75	6.5
08 July 1949	14.00	-91.50	6.0
17 Feb 1950	14.50	-90.00	6.4
23 Oct 1950	14.50	-92.00	7.3
23 Oct 1950	13.80	-91.78	6.5
23 Oct 1950	13.80	-91.78	6.5
23 Oct 1950	14.50	-92.00	6.1
24 Oct 1950	14.50	-92.00	6.2
24 Oct 1950	13.80	-91.78	6.0
05 Nov 1950	14.00	-92.40	6.5
25 July 1951	21.00	-91.38	6.2
24 Aug 1953	13.60	-91.90	6.8
17 Nov 1953	13.80	-91.80	7.4
21 Oct 1954	14.00	-90.50	6.5
26 Apr 1955	13.50	-89.50	6.5

28 Aug 1955	13.80	-91.78	6.8
03 Sep 1955	14.00	-91.00	6.6
11 Sep 1956	14.00	-91.00	6.1
04 Dec 1956	15.00	-92.00	6.0
08 July 1957	14.50	-91.00	6.0
24 Jan 1959	15.00	-92.50	6.2
20 Feb 1959	15.50	-91.00	6.5
09 Mar 1959	15.50	-91.00	6.3
13 Apr 1960	15.50	-92.00	6.0
20 Aug 1960	14.75	-91.75	6.0
14 June 1961	13.80	-91.78	6.0
17 June 1961	14.60	-92.10	6.0
01 Sep 1961	13.60	-92.50	6.5
18 Aug 1966	14.60	-91.80	6.0
21 Apr 1969	14.00	-91.30	6.0
31 Dec 1974	14.13	-91.82	6.1
04 Feb 1976	15.30	-89.10	7.5
06 Feb 1976	15.00	-90.90	6.2
27 Oct 1979	13.78	-90.73	6.6
09 Aug 1980	15.89	-88.52	6.4
06 Apr 1982	14.31	-92.08	6.5
19 June 1982	16.10	-90.80	6.5
03 June 1985	13.50	-90.30	6.4
24 Mar 1986	14.33	-91.72	6.5
07 Apr 1986	14.70	-91.90	6.1
18 June 1988	13.85	-90.70	6.1
25 Mar 1990	17.91	-89.12	6.3
28 Apr 1990	15.27	-88.09	6.0
14 Mar 1994	16.68	-93.36	6.1
04 Nov 1996	12.82	-89.67	6.2
11 July 1999	15.89	-87.99	6.1
13 Jan 2001	12.75	-88.85	7.0

(m = Mercalli scale)

Adapted from "Chronological Historical Record of Damaging Earthquakes in Guatemala, 1526-1976" published by the U.S. Government Printing Office (1976-0-211/167) and information provided by the Meteorological Institute in Guatemala City (INSIVUMEH).

Eruptions

Recorded Fuego Eruptions

1524 – Eruption
1526 – Moderate eruption
1541 – Moderate activity
1575 – Moderate activity
1576 – Eruption of ash and gases
1577 – light activity
December 27, 1581 – Major eruption of ash
July to Dec 1585 – Ash eruption
March 1586 – Moderate eruption
1614 – Moderate eruption
January, 1623 – Strong activity, rumbling
1631 – Moderate activity
1632 – Light eruption
1651 – Eruption of ash
1664 – Light activity
1668 – Light activity
1671 – Moderate eruption
1677 – Moderate activity
1685 – Moderate activity (?)
1689 – Doubtful eruption
1699 – Eruption of lava
February 1-2, 1705 – Ash eruption
October 4, 1706 – Activity of ash and gases
October 15, 1710 – Eruption of ash
August to December, 1717 – Strong eruption of ash
May, 1732 – Moderate eruption
August 27, 1737 – Eruption of ash (lateral crater)
1751 – Light activity
1773 – Moderate activity
1775 – Moderate activity
1799 – Eruption of ash
1829 – Moderate eruption
1852 – Surprise eruption
October, 1852 – Activity of ash and lava
September 28, 1855 – Eruption of ash, lava and smoke

1856 – Eruption of ash and lava
March to November, 1856 – Immense amount of water vapor
January, March 9-10, 1857 – Unrestrained lava
August – September, 1860 – Ash and lava activity
1861 – Light activity
June, August, September 1880 – Activity with rumbling
1896 – Notable eruption
1930 – Doubtful eruption
February, 1932 – Very strong eruption, large amount of ash
1944 – Strong eruption of ash and lava
October, 1944– Moderate eruption
December, 1947 – Light activity
May, 1953 – Intense smoking
May, 1954 – Intense smoking
July, 1955 – Light activity with ash
September, 1955 – Light activity with ash
August, November, 1962 – Eruption with ash and lava
September, 1963 – Moderate activity with ash
1967 – Light activity with ash
July, 1969 – Light activity
November, 1970 – Light activity
January, 1972 – Some activity with ash
October, 1974 – Strong activity with large amounts of ash
1975 – Eruption of ash and gas
November, 1975 – Short moderate eruption
January, 1977 – Micro eruption
April to May, 1977 – Eruption of gases
August 1977 – Gases and water vapor
September, 1977 – Eruption of gases and ash
November to December, 1977 – Light activity with ash
2000 – Large and small explosions of ash with rumbling
2002 – Volcanic activity increased on January 4th. In February, lava was observed flowing down the east side of the crater and formed a dome inside it, which has been almost completely filled. After another increase of activity on February 9th, the lava flow descended Las Lajas. The flow reached appoximately 1,500 meters. A cone was formed inside the crater, with a height of 30–50 meters.

Translated from information obtained from the Meteorological Institute in Guatemala City (INSIVUMEH).

Bibliography

Annis, Verle L. *The Architecture of Antigua Guatemala 1543–1773*. Guatemala: Universidad de San Carlos, 1968.

Aycinena Echeverría, Roberto. "Generalidades sobre la Arquitectura de la Antigua Guatemala". *Carta Informativa del CNPAG*, Guatemala, Año VIII, N° 1, enero/febrero, 1981.

Barascout Corcuera, Enrique. *Puesta en Valor del Conjunto de la Compañía de Jesús para Centro Cultural de la Antigua Guatemala*. Tesis Arquitectura. Guatemala: Universidad de San Carlos, 1979.

Bell, Elizabeth y Trevor Long. *Antigua Guatemala*. Guatemala: Filmtrek, 1978.

Carta Informativa del Consejo Nacional Para la Protección de La Antigua Guatemala. Guatemala: Consejo Nacional para la Protección de La Antigua Guatemala, Guatemala, 1972–1986.

Cortés y Larraz, Pedro. *Descripción Geográfico-moral de la Diócesis de Goathemala* 2 tomos. Guatemala: Biblioteca "Goathemala" de la Sociedad de Geografía e Historia. Vol. XX. 1958.

De las Casas, Bartolomé. *Breve Relación de la Destrucción de las Indias Occidentales: presentada a Felipe II siendo príncipe de Asturias*. México: Libros Luciérnaga, 1957.

Díaz del Castillo, Bernal. *Verdadera y Notable Relación del Descubrimiento y Conquista de la Nueva España y Guatemala*. Tomo I, ed. 1933; Tomo II, ed. 1934. Guatemala: Biblioteca "Goathemala" de la Sociedad de Geografía e Historia. Vol. X–XI.

Dombrowski, John y otros. *Area Handbook for Guatemala*. Washington, D.C.: U.S. Government Printing Office, 1970.

Gage, Tomás. *Nueva Relación Que Contiene Los Viajes de Tomás Gage en la Nueva España*. Guatemala: Editorial "José de Pineda Ibarra", 1979.

Fuentes y Guzmán, Francisco Antonio de. *Recordación Florida. Discurso Historial y Demostración Natural, Material y Política del Reyno de Guatemala*. Tomo I, 1932; Tomo II, 1933; Tomo III, 1933. Guatemala: Biblioteca "Goathemala" de la Sociedad de Geografía e Historia. Vol. VI – VIII.

179

García de Cuevas, Natalia. *El Arte Popular de la Cerería en Guatemala*. Guatemala: Sub-Centro Regional de Artesanías y Artes Populares, 1983.

Galicia Díaz, Julio. *Destrucción y Traslado de la Ciudad de Santiago de Guatemala*. Guatemala: Editorial Universitaria, 1976.

García Laguardia, Jorge Mario y Jorge Luján Muñoz. *Guía de Técnicas de Investigación y Cuaderno de Trabajo*. 19ª Edición. Guatemala: Serviprensa, 1988.

García López, Benjamín. "Datos Folklóricos y Monográficos de Algunas Aldeas y Municipios de Antigua y Sacatepéquez Respectivamente". Guatemala: s.e., 1977.

González R., Mario Gilberto. *Distinciones Otorgadas a la Muy Noble y Muy Leal Ciudad de Santiago de los Caballeros de Guatemala*. Guatemala: Editorial "José de Pineda Ibarra", 1964.

Herrera M., J. Francisco. *Leyendas Antigüeñas*. Guatemala: Artes Gráficas "Amil", s.f.

Hibbitts, John E. *Estado de Conservación de las Iglesias de Antigua Guatemala*. Guatemala: Editorial Universitaria, 1968.

János de Szécsy. *Santiago de los Caballeros de Goathemala, en Almolonga; investigaciones del año 1950*. Traducción al español por Yolanda de Oreamuno. Guatemala: Editorial del Ministerio de Educación Pública, 1953.

Jickling, David L. *La Ciudad de Santiago de Guatemala: por sus cronistas y viajeros*. La Antigua Guatemala: Centro de Investigaciones Regionales de Mesoamérica, 1987.

Jickling, David y Elaine D. Elliott. *Façades and Festivals of Antigua: a Guide to Church Fronts and Celebrations*. Guatemala: s.e., 1989.

Jil Salomé. *Los Nazarenos*. 3ª Reimpresión. Guatemala: Editorial Piedra Santa, 1991.

Kéléman, Pal. "Colonial Architecture in Guatemala". *Bulletin of the Pan American Union*, Vol. LXXV, Nº 8, August, 1941.

Kelsey, Harry. *Juan Rodríguez Cabrillo*. San Marino: Huntington Library, 1986.

Lamadrid, Lázaro. *Extracto de la Guía Turística de San Francisco en Antigua Guatemala*. Guatemala: Tipografía Nacional, 1962.

Lehnhoff, Dieter. *Música de la Epoca Colonial en Guatemala*. La Antigua Guatemala: Centro de Investigaciones Regionales de Mesoamérica, 1984.

Ley Protectora de la Antigua Guatemala. Reglamentos y Normas Relacionados a la Protección del Conjunto Monumental. Guatemala: Consejo Nacional para la Protección de la Antigua Guatemala, 1972.

Libro Viejo de la Fundación de Guatemala. Edición crítica Carmelo Sáenz de Santa María. Guatemala: Academia de Geografía e Historia de Guatemala, 1991.

Lovell, W. George. *Conquest and Survival in Colonial Guatemala. A Historical Geography of the Cuchumatán Highlands 1500–1821*. Kingston and Montreal: McGill-Queen's University Press, 1985.

Lovell, W. George. *Life and Death in Guatemala*. Toronto: Between the Lines, 1995.

Luján Muñoz, Jorge. *El Monasterio de Nuestra Señora del Pilar de Zaragoza de Guatemala (1720–1874)*. Tesis Humanidades. Guatemala: Universidad de San Carlos, 1963.

Luján Muñoz, Jorge. *Permanencia de Antigua*. Guatemala: Universidad de San Carlos, 1966.

Luján Muñoz, Jorge. *Guía del Convento de Capuchinas de Antigua Guatemala*. Guatemala: Editorial "José de Pineda Ibarra", 1977.

Luján Muñoz, Jorge. *Inicios del Dominio Español en Indias*. Guatemala: Editorial Universitaria, 1987.

Luján Muñoz, Luis. *La Plaza Mayor de Santiago de Guatemala hacia 1678*. Guatemala: Instituto de Antropología e Historia (Publicación especial Nº 3), 1969.

Luján Muñoz, Luis. *Síntesis de la Arquitectura en Guatemala*. 2ª Impresión. Guatemala: Universidad de San Carlos, 1972.

Luján Muñoz, Luis. *Lybro de Cocyna: Que Contiene el Modo de Hacer los Pucheros, Sopas, Guizos, Nogadas, Salsas, Tortas, Pasteles, Marquezotes, Quezadias, Dulces, Tamales, Tamalitos, Pastelitos, Biscotelas, y Otras Cosas*. Guatemala: Universidad de San Carlos, Centro de Estudios Folklóricos, 1972.

Luján Muñoz, Luis. *Historia de la Mayólica en Guatemala*. Guatemala: Instituto de Antropología e Historia, 1975.

Luján Muñoz, Luis. *Síntesis Biográfica del Maestro Mayor de Arquitectura Diego de Porres (1677–1977)*. La Antigua Guatemala: Consejo Nacional para la Protección de La Antigua Guatemala, 1977.

Luján Muñoz, Luis. *Fuentes de Antigua Guatemala*. 2ª Edición. Guatemala: Editorial "José de Pineda Ibarra", 1991.

Luján Muñoz, Luis. "Breve Perfil de la Vida y la Obra de Bernal Díaz del Castillo". *Carta Informativa del CNPAG*, Guatemala, Año XI Nº 3, marzo/abril 1984.

Luján Muñoz, Luis. *Fotografías de Eduardo Santiago Muybridge en Guatemala (1875)*. Guatemala: Cenaltex, 1984.

Luján Muñoz, Luis. "Algo sobre Arqueología Histórica en Antigua Guatemala" *Carta Informativa del CNPAG*, Guatemala, Año VIII Nº 3, mayo/junio 1981.

Lutz, Christopher H. *Santiago de Guatemala 1541–1773. City, Caste, and the Colonial Experience*. Norman and London: University of Oklahoma Press, 1994.

Magaña Juárez, José María. "El Deterioro de los Monumentos de la Antigua Guatemala y Su Reestructuración". *Carta Informativa del CNPAG*, Guatemala, Año XII no. 3, mayo/junio 1986.

Markman, Sidney David. *Architecture and Urbanization of Colonial Central America*. Vol. I. Primary Documentary and Literary Sources. Tempe: Center for Latin American Studies, Arizona State University, 1993.

Markman, Sidney David. *Colonial Architecture of Antigua Guatemala*. Philadelphia: American Philosophical Society, 1966.

Martínez Peláez, Severo. *La Patria del Criollo*. México: Ediciones en Marcha, 1990.

Mata Gavidia, José. *Anotaciones de Historia Patria Centroamericana*. Guatemala: Editorial Universitaria, 1969.

Memoria de Labores del Consejo Nacional Para la Protección de la Antigua Guatemala. Guatemala: Consejo Nacional para la Protección de La Antigua Guatemala, 1972–1988.

Pardo, José Joaquín, Pedro Zamora Castellanos y Luis Luján Muñoz. *Guía de La Antigua Guatemala*. 3ª Edición. Sociedad de Geografía e Historia. Guatemala: Editorial "José de Pineda Ibarra", 1969.

Pardo, José Joaquín. *Efemérides de Antigua Guatemala 1541–1779*. 3ª Edición. La Antigua Guatemala: Consejo Nacional para la Protección de La Antigua Guatemala, 1984.

Popenoe, Dorothy H. *Santiago de los Caballeros de Guatemala*. Cambridge: Harvard University Press, 1933.

Popenoe, Wilson. "La Casa del Oidor. Santiago de los Caballeros de Guatemala". Honduras: Imprenta Soto, s.f.

Price, Nicholas Stanley, M. Kirby Talley Jr., and Alessandra Melucco Vaccaro, eds. *Historical and Philosophical Issues in the Conservation of Cultural Heritage*. Los Angeles: The Getty Conservation Institute, 1996.

Prober, Kurt. *Historia Numismática de Guatemala*. 2ª Edición. Guatemala: J.L. Arriola, 1973.

Remesal, Fray Antonio de. *Historia General de Las Indias Occidentales, y Particular de La Gobernación de Chiapa y Guatemala*. 2ª Edición. 2 tomos. Guatemala: Biblioteca "Goathemala" de la Sociedad de Geografía e Historia. Vol. IV–V. 1932.

Rubio Sánchez, Manuel. *El Real Palacio de la Ciudad de Santiago de Guatemala*. Guatemala: Editorial "José de Pineda Ibarra", 1976.

Rubio Sánchez, Manuel. *Historial del Ayuntamiento de la Ciudad de Antigua Guatemala*. Guatemala: Academia de Geografía e Historia, 1983.

Rubio Sánchez, Manuel. *Monografía de la Ciudad de Antigua Guatemala*. Guatemala: Tipografía Nacional, 1989.

Samayoa Guevara, Héctor Humberto. *Los Gremios de Artesanos en la Ciudad de Guatemala 1524–1821*. Guatemala: Piedra Santa, 1978.

Shawcross, Mike. *Antigua, Guatemala. City and Area Guide*. Guatemala: Serviprensa, 1979.

Shook, Edwin M. *Incidents in the Life of a Maya Archaeologist. As Told to Winifred Veronda*. Guatemala: Asociación de Amigos del País y Fundación para la Cultura y el Desarrollo, 1998.

Swezey, William R. "La Evolución Arquitectónica de la Capilla de la Tercera Orden de la Penitencia de la Iglesia de San Francisco el Grande de la Antigua Guatemala y de los varios entierros del Venerable Hermano Pedro de San José de Betancur". *Carta Informativa del CNPAG*, Guatemala, Año XV, Nº 5, Septiembre/octubre, 1984.

To Quiñónez, Marco Antonio. *Antigua: Mito y Realidad: contribución a un análisis crítico*. Tesis Arquitectura. Guatemala: Universidad de San Carlos, 1976.

Vásquez, R. P. Fray Francisco. *Crónica de la Provincia del Santísimo Nombre de Jesús de Guatemala; de la Orden de N. Seráfico Padre San Francisco en el Reino de la Nueva España* Tomo I, ed. 1937; Tomo II, ed. 1938; Tomo III, ed. 1940; Tomo IV, ed. 1944. Guatemala: Bibliografía "Goathemala" de la Sociedad de Geografía e Historia. Vols. XIV–XVII.

U.S. Government Printing Office. "Chronological Historical Record of Damaging Earthquakes in Guatemala, 1526–1976". Washington D.C.: U.S. Government Printing Office, 1976.

Woodward, Ralph Lee. *Central America*. New York: Oxford University Press, 1976.

Ximénez, Francisco (Fray). *Historia de la Provincia de San Vicente de Chiapa y Guatemala de la Orden de Predicadores*. Tomo I, ed. 1929; Tomo II, ed. 1930; Tomo III, ed. 1931. Guatemala: Biblioteca "Goathemala" de la Sociedad de Geografía e Historia. Vol. I–III.

Yas, J. J. and J. D. Noriega. *La Antigua Guatemala*. Buenos Aires: La Azotea, 1990.

Zavala, Silvio. *Contribución a la Historia de las Instituciones Coloniales en Guatemala*. 1ª Reimpresión. Guatemala: Editorial Universitaria, 1986.

Zilbermann de Luján, Cristina. *Aspectos Socio-económicos del Traslado de la Ciudad de Guatemala, 1773–1783*. Guatemala: Academia de Geografía e Historia de Guatemala, 1987.

Map

Antigua Guatemala Map

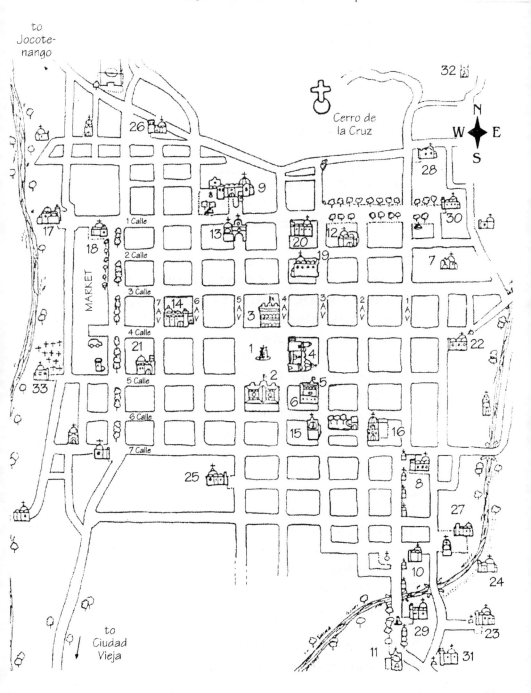

Monuments

1- Main Square

2- Palace of the Captains General

3- City Hall Palace

4- Cathedral and Archbishop's Palace

5- Old University of San Carlos
   Museum of Colonial Art

6- Tridentino Seminary and Schools

7- Santo Domingo Church and Monastery

8- San Francisco Church and Monastery
   Santo Hermano Pedro Museum

9- La Merced Church and Monastery

10- Escuela de Cristo Church

11- El Calvario Church

12- Capuchinas Church and Convent

13- Santa Catalina Church, Convent and Arch

14- Compañía de Jesús Church and Monastery

15- Hermano Pedro Hospital

16- Santa Clara Church and Convent

17- La Recolección Church and Monastery

18- San Jerónimo Royal Customhouse

19- El Carmen Church and Convent

20- Santa Teresa Church and Convent

21- San Agustín Church and Convent

22- La Concepción Church and Convent

23- Santa Ana Church

24- Santa Cruz Hermitage

25- San José el Viejo Hermitage

26- San Sebastián Church

27- Belén School and Churches

28- La Candelaria Church

29- Los Remedios Church

30- Santa Rosa de Lima Church

31- Santa Isabel Hermitage

32- Los Dolores del Cerro Church

33- San Lázaro Church and Cemetery